Practical Guide to
Advanced DSOs in SAP®

Deepa Rawat

Thank you for purchasing this book from Espresso Tutorials!

Like a cup of espresso coffee, Espresso Tutorials SAP books are concise and effective. We know that your time is valuable and we deliver information in a succinct and straightforward manner. It only takes our readers a short amount of time to consume SAP concepts. Our books are well recognized in the industry for leveraging tutorial-style instruction and videos to show you step by step how to successfully work with SAP.

Check out our YouTube channel to watch our videos at
https://www.youtube.com/user/EspressoTutorials.

If you are interested in SAP Finance and Controlling, join us at
http://www.fico-forum.com/forum2/
to get your SAP questions answered and contribute to discussions.

Related titles from Espresso Tutorials:

▶ Anurag Barua: First Steps in SAP® Crystal Reports for Business Users
  http://5017.espresso-tutorials.com

▶ Wolfgang Niefert: Business Intelligence with SAP® BI Edge
  http://4040.espresso-tutorials.com

▶ Paul Ovigele: Reconciling SAP® CO-PA to the General Ledger
  http://5040.espresso-tutorials.com

▶ Kermit Bravo & Scott Cairncross: SAP® Enterprise Performance Management (EPM) Add-In *http://5042.espresso-tutorials.com*

▶ Gerardo di Giuseppe: First Steps in SAP® Business Warehouse (BW)
  http://5088.espresso-tutorials.com

▶ Jörg Böke: SAP® BI Analysis Office – a Practical Guide
  http://5096.espresso-tutorials.com

▶ Shreekant Shiralkar & Deepak Sawant: SAP® BW Performance Optimization *http://5102.espresso-tutorials.com*

▶ Christian Savelli: SAP® BW on SAP HANA
  http://5128.espresso-tutorials.com

▶ Frank Riesner, Klaus-Peter Sauer: First Steps in SAP® FI Configuration
  http://5215.espresso-tutorials.com

Deepa Rawat
Practical Guide to Advanced DSOs in SAP®

ISBN:	978-1-71885-302-7
Editor:	Lisa Jackson
Cover Design:	Philip Esch
Cover Photo:	istockphoto.com | chrispecoraro No. 183043557
Interior Book Design:	Johann-Christian Hanke

All rights reserved.

1st Edition 2018, Gleichen

© 2018 by Espresso Tutorials GmbH

URL: *www.espresso-tutorials.com*

Feedback
We greatly appreciate any kind of feedback you have concerning this book. Please mail us at *info@espresso-tutorials.com*.

Table of Contents

Preface

This book introduces you to the basic concepts of the Advanced Data Store Object (aDSO) within SAP BW on SAP HANA. It discusses, in detail, the various aDSO templates that SAP has provided. With the help of each template, you can quickly create your own aDSO specific to the business need. Apart from the templates, this book also discusses all the additional features that the aDSOs come with. aDSOs cannot be used on their own. They require knowledge of embedding the aDSOs within composite providers and require knowledge of creating queries on the composite providers using SAP HANA Studio. There are two examples at the end of this book that will show you how to use the templates, will help you understand how to embed the aDSOs within queries, and will help you create your first query quickly using field-based modeling. InfoObject-based modeling is also shown. This book covers these topics and more! Enjoy reading this book!

Acknowledgements:

This book is dedicated to my parents, Ravi and Mridula, who have always encouraged me to think big and have always inspired me to follow my dreams. They have always believed in me and have emotionally supported me in everything I do. To my husband, Surya, thank you for listening to all my complaints and offering me advice when I wanted it. Without your patience, this book could not have been completed. Thank you for reading through the entire book and helping me fix my grammar and spelling mistakes. Thank you to my children, Sneha and Roma, for encouraging me all along. The fictitious names (for creating examples in the book), editing advice, and silent road trip while I wrote the book all helped on the journey to completing my first book. Thanks to my sister Jaya, my brother Vikram, and my sister-in-law Shruti, for always pointing me in the right direction and always encouraging me with positive feedback about my career.

I must also thank Espresso Tutorials for giving me the opportunity to write this book. Without their help, this book would not have been possible.

We have added a few icons to highlight important information. These include:

Tips

Tips highlight information that provides more details about the subject being described and/or additional background information.

Attention

Attention notices highlight information that you should be aware of when you go through the examples in this book on your own.

Finally, a note concerning the copyright: all screenshots printed in this book are the copyright of SAP SE. All rights are reserved by SAP SE. Copyright pertains to all SAP images in this publication. For the sake of simplicity, we do not mention this specifically underneath every screen-shot.

1 Data warehousing and database technologies

Over a period of time, enterprises collect a lot of data to run their organizations. Managers are always trying to gather this data and make sense out of it; they try to analyze the data to understand how their product is doing compared to their competitor. For managers to do their analysis, the technology department creates databases and creates SQL queries to evaluate the data stored in the databases and then publish the SQL queries so business users can run reports when they need information about their products. When the database grows in size, IT departments need special techniques to organize the data such that the database size is lean and queries take less time to return a response.

Regular relational databases are good for storing data and processing transactional data (OLTP—online transactional processing), but when it comes to retrieving this data and performing analysis on it, special "warehousing" techniques are needed (OLAP—online analytical processing). Data warehousing is a collection of tools, methods, and database techniques that help support the decision makers of an organization such that they can analyze their own company's data and make the right decision at the right time.

In an enterprise, data is usually collected by each division by different methods. Every division might have its own clever way of collecting and managing its operational data. It becomes a challenge to integrate this data, as each division could use different software to manage its transaction data. Data warehousing tools help to extract data from different software platforms and store it in a unified form on a software platform that is more suitable for reporting. An operational database is a live database platform where data gets collected every second of the day. On the other hand, data warehouses collect data at intervals from an OLTP database. It is more a snapshot-based system than an online system.

Some of the differences between an OLTP system and OLAP system are shown in Figure 1.1.

Feature	Operational Databases	Data Warehouses
Users	Thousands	Hundreds
Workload	Preset transactions	Specific analysis queries
Access	To hundreds of records, write and read mode	To millions of records, mainly read-only mode
Goal	Depends on applications	Decision-making support
Data	Detailed, both numeric and alphanumeric	Summed up, mainly numeric
Data integration	Application-based	Subject-based
Quality	In terms of integrity	In terms of consistency
Time coverage	Current data only	Current and historical data
Updates	Continuous	Periodical
Model	Normalized	Denormalized, multidimensional
Optimization	For OLTP access to a database part	For OLAP access to most of the database

Figure 1.1: Differences between OLTP and OLAP systems

To bring this topic into the context of SAP, SAP is an enterprise resource planning (ERP) system that corresponds to an OLTP system. The tool, SAP, helps collect transactional data within an organization. SAP Business Warehouse (BW), now known as Business Intelligence, is a module within the SAP system that helps managers perform analysis on the data that resides within the ERP system. The SAP BW module usually resides on a separate server, extracts relevant data from the ERP system and other source systems, and houses the data into a separate OLAP database. The OLTP system is created to provide efficient database storage capacity, whereas OLAP databases are created to provide efficient querying or reporting capabilities.

These efficient reporting features within the OLAP databases are created by utilizing either the starflake schema or the snowflake schema. These schemas are discussed in more detail in the next section.

1.1   Starflake schema vs. snowflake schema

There are usually two ways to design tables in an OLAP database system:

- ▶ Starflake schema
- ▶ Snowflake schema

Starflake schema

Starflake schema is a database schema that looks like a simple star. It has a central table with the facts (key figures or numbers) and multiple dimension tables connected to the central table with the help of primary and foreign key relationships. A sample is shown in Figure 1.2. This sample has the central table with the order data. The central table is surrounded by small tables that hold more information about the key figures.

Look at the example in Figure 1.2. The key figures are held in the central table called ORDER DATA. The two key figures are ORDER VOLUME and ORDER VALUE. These two key figures are then identified using characteristics like customer ID, material number, sales organization ID, and other IDs. These are only the codes or IDs. The descriptive part of the codes is maintained in the surrounding dimension tables. This sort of storing is done so that the master data fields, such as text and other attributes, can be easily edited for a code. This schema gives flexibility to a reporting tool as these tables can be quickly combined and presented for reporting.

Material Data

Material Number	CHAR	18
Material Short Description	CHAR	20
Material Medium Description	CHAR	40
Material Long Description	CHAR	60

Division

Division	CHAR	2
Division Short Description	CHAR	20

Distr. Channel

Distribution Channel	CHAR	4
Division Short Description	CHAR	20

Order Data

Order Document Number	CHAR	10
Order Item Number	CHAR	6
Customer Number	CHAR	10
Material Number	CHAR	18
Sales Organization	CHAR	4
Divison	CHAR	2
Distribution Channel	CHAR	2
Order Volume	NUMC	17,2
Order value	NUMC	17,2

Customer Data

Customer Number	CHAR	10
Customer Short Description	CHAR	20
Customer Medium Description	CHAR	40
Customer Long Description	CHAR	60

Sales Org

Sales Organization	CHAR	4
Sales Org Short Description	CHAR	20
Sales Org Medium Description	CHAR	40
Sales Org Long Description	CHAR	60

Figure 1.2: Starflake schema

Snowflake schema

Snowflake schema also has a central fact table, but instead of the single layer of surrounding tables, it has dimension tables connected to multiple subdimension tables as shown in Figure 1.3.

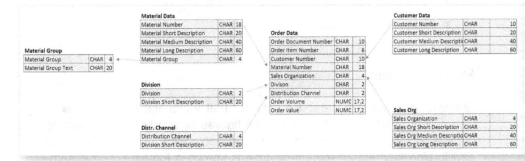

Figure 1.3: Snowflake schema

In Figure 1.3, MATERIAL DATA is further connected to the subdimension table MATERIAL GROUP. Some OLAP engines are better suited to read snowflake schemas than starflake schemas. As data warehousing needs are complex in nature, it is not always possible to have an exact starflake schema for each report. SAP BW is an example of an extended starflake schema.

1.2 Relational databases and SAP HANA

A database is a means of storing information digitally such that it can be retrieved later for reporting purposes. Tables are objects within a database that is used to store related pieces of information. For example, order data is usually kept in one table. The programming language commonly used to retrieve data from database tables is called SQL. SQL is a universal language that is used by all database systems.

SAP HANA is an in-memory, column-oriented relational database management system that was created by SAP. It can be used for OLTP as well as OLAP, hence it is also known as an OLTAP database system.

▶ In-memory—SAP HANA is an in-memory database system. It is called in-memory because it stores data in the main memory instead of on storage disks. This increases the reporting performance as no time is spent accessing database disks to retrieve data. Storing all the transactional data in main memory requires a large in-memory space, which can be very costly with respect to data storage. SAP came up with the concept that since 85% of data in an ERP environment is usually not needed or is accessed infrequently, it can be cost effective to store the needed data or "hot" data in-memory and store the infrequently accessed data, also called "warm" data, on disks. SAP also calls this dynamic tiering.

▶ Column-oriented—SAP HANA is a column-oriented database. Traditionally, all data related to a row is stored by relational database systems in a row. SAP HANA, on the other hand, stores all data related to a column in the same memory space. Typically, for reporting, this can be very efficient. If a report has a column that needs displaying, the database would not need to go to different places to fetch data. It can go to one spot in-memory and fetch all column-related data at once. This can result in a high degree of performance enhancement.

1.3   SAP BW on SAP HANA

When the SAP BW software is set up on an SAP HANA database, it is known as SAP BW on SAP HANA. SAP BW, traditionally, has been installed on several different relational databases, such as Oracle, DB2, etc., but SAP now recommends changing the database to SAP HANA. This is because the SAP BW software for SAP HANA comes with a very efficient data-modeling tool and metadata objects that cannot be created on traditional relational databases.

When SAP BW is run on SAP HANA, it gives the following advantages:

▶ Elimination of SAP BW accelerator—Traditionally, SAP BW required a database and a separate SAP BW accelerator. When InfoCubes contained a large amount of data, a separate accelerator or indexing mechanism was needed to help queries return faster results. Now, with SAP HANA, you can have both features provided by the same tool. There is no need for two types of databases and managing tools; everything can be managed by one SAP HANA database.

▶ With SAP HANA, OLTP and OLAP databases can be merged. You do not need one database for OLTP and another one for OLAP anymore. Tables in the OLTP database can be exposed to SAP BW on SAP HANA via SAP HANA views. The SAP HANA views can then be used to view data in SAP BW either via Open ODS views or composite providers.

▶ SAP BW on SAP HANA has made some of the persistence layers obsolete. It provides unique modeling for creating Advanced DSOs. This has made persistent staging areas (PSAs) and other types of objects redundant.

▶ Traditionally, when transformations were executed, they were executed in-memory. But now, these transformations can be pushed to the database (database-managed procedures) for a quicker turnaround. Hence data loads can now take less time on an SAP HANA database.

▶ Activation of load requests is now faster as the activation process is pushed to the SAP HANA database.

▶ SAP BW on SAP HANA only needs four different modeling objects:

  ▶ InfoObjects
  ▶ Advanced DSOs
  ▶ Open ODS views
  ▶ Composite providers

SAP BW on other databases needs a lot more objects to create reports. The list of objects that need to be created for the third-party databases are shown next. This list is a summary of different types of objects possible in an SAP BW environment. This is not an all-inclusive list.

▶ InfoObjects—InfoObjects are the smallest building blocks in SAP BW. These help evaluate the business needs.

▶ Persistent staging area (PSA)—PSA is the set of inbound staging tables, where data is collected from different source systems.

▶ Classic DSOs—Classic DSOs are a set of tables where data is collected, staged, and cleansed before it is sent for reporting.

▶ InfoCube—This is a datatarget that can be used to stage a data to feed another datatarget; it can also be used for reporting.

▶ Virtual provider—This is an object in SAP BW where data is not stored. It can only be used for reporting.

▶ InfoSet—InfoSets are views that join different types of datatargets together for reporting or for feeding data to other data targets.

▶ Multiprovider—Multiprovider is a way to combine different datatargets (by using the concept of union) and make data available for reporting.

▶ Hybrid provider—Hybrid provider is an alternate way of reporting. This provider shows real-time data.

▶ Composite provider (third-party version)—Composite provider is an object in SAP BW that combines data, either using joins or unions, to make data available for reporting.

1.4 LSA and LSA++ architecture

The term LSA stands for layered scalable architecture. This type of architecture enables a structured way to build an enterprise-wide data warehouse. A data warehouse needs to be designed so that it is scalable and structured. SAP BW systems are usually designed with the concept of LSA in mind.

1.4.1 LSA architecture

The LSA architecture (as published by SAP on help.sap.com) is shown in Figure 1.4.

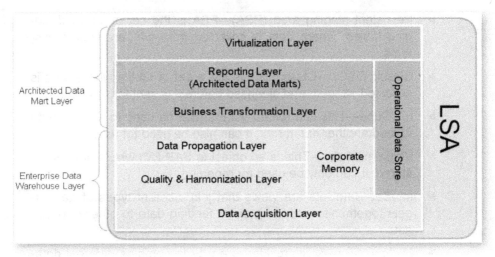

Figure 1.4: LSA architecture

The LSA architecture consists of two main layers: the enterprise data warehouse (EDW) layer and the architected datamart (ADM) layer.

The EDW layer consists of the following four layers:

Data acquisition layer (DAL) is the layer that acquires data from various source systems. Data can be acquired from different databases and flatfiles and stored in this layer.

Quality and harmonization layer (QHL) is the layer that acquires data from the data acquisition layer and cleanses data and converts data into the EDW format. For example, if the code needs to be 18 characters instead of 10, then this conversion to a standard format is done in this layer.

Data propagation layer (DPL) is the layer that can utilize the data in the QHL and create semantic groups. Semantic groups might be needed in some data warehouses to split data by country, region, or year. The conversions can be done in this layer. If the conversions are not needed, this layer can be skipped.

Corporate memory (CM) is where data is acquired from the DAL and kept in a manner to preserve history. This layer can be utilized to reconstruct data, when needed.

The architected datamart (ADM) layer consists of the following four layers:

Business transformation layer (BTL) is the layer where data is acquired from the DPL and converted into business terminology. This is usually stored in classic DSOs. For example, a key figure that is a complex calculation of some other key figures acquired from the source system needs to be created. This layer could also be utilized to create additional characteristics based on basic characteristics acquired from the source.

Reporting layer (RL) is where data is assembled into InfoCubes, multiproviders, InfoSets, virtual providers, or composite providers by combining data from the various containers in the BTL.

Virtualization layer (VL) is where queries are created to utilize structures created in the RL and for business users to access their data.

Operational datastore layer (ODL) is the layer that stores very granular data. Usually, by the time data is moved to the RL, data is extremely summarized in nature. If the business wants to drill down to the details of the summarized data, queries can be built on top of the ODL to support summarized queries.

The LSA architecture was utilized to build SAP BW environments before the SAP HANA database came into being. Once the SAP HANA database was introduced, LSA was replaced by LSA++ because of simplification introduced by the objects that SAP HANA needed to deliver fast queries.

1.4.2   LSA++ architecture

The LSA++ architecture (as published by SAP on help.sap.com) is shown in Figure 1.5.

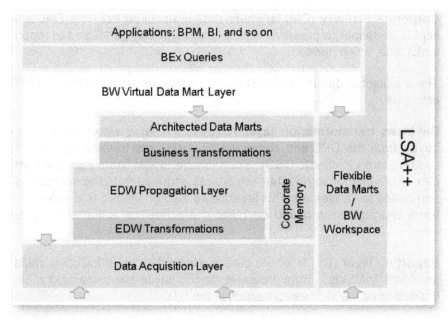

Figure 1.5: LSA++ architecture

The LSA++ architecture contains the same EDW layer as LSA. The main difference is introduced with the flexible reporting layer in LSA++. This flexibility has been introduced by the Advanced DSOs available in SAP BW on an SAP HANA database. The BW queries can now:

▶ Flexibly access data in the DAL (if the DAL is made up of Advanced DSOs suited for this layer)

▶ Flexibly access data in the BTL and ADM layer as these layers can now be made up of Advanced DSOs modeled to suit this layer.

▶ Flexibly access the SAP HANA database because of availability of transient and virtual providers that allow for such access to queries.

2 New objects in SAP BW and SAP HANA

Creating a data warehouse using SAP BW takes time because of InfoObject-based modeling technologies. In order to extract data into the older version of SAP BW (version 3.x or before), every source field that needed extraction into SAP BW had to be converted into an InfoObject in SAP BW before a simple report could be created. With SAP BW 7.4 and SAP BW 7.5 on SAP HANA, SAP has introduced field-based modeling and has brought in robust virtual objects. You can now implement reportable objects that do not need InfoObjects. This has changed the speed with which a data warehouse can be implemented.

Some of the new features that have been introduced with SAP BW 7.5 on SAP HANA are:

► Open ODS views

► Composite providers

► Advanced DSOs

There are many more new features, but these are the only objects discussed in this book.

2.1 Open ODS views

In SAP BW, modelers create reports that are meant to return results in a short amount of time. To do this, extensive modeling efforts are required to produce the reports. These modeling efforts require creating complex data models in SAP BW, which are time-consuming. Regular SAP BW modeling requires creating InfoObjects of type characteristics and key figures that are in turn used in InfoProviders and queries to return results.

Open ODS view was introduced when SAP released SAP BW 7.4 SP5 on SAP HANA. An Open ODS view allows SAP to integrate external tables and views (on external databases) with SAP BW's transaction and master data by utilizing a view concept. As this interface is a view-based interface, it means that an Open ODS view allows external data to be integrated within SAP BW without data persistency. An Open ODS view can provide three types of semantics within SAP BW. It can enable the external table structures within SAP BW as facts, attributes, or texts. Open ODS views help deliver reports in a shorter amount of time. Unlike other InfoProviders in SAP BW (classic DSOs, InfoCubes, etc.), they do not require InfoObjects for their creation; instead, they use fields for defining the construct of the view. Hence, they are field-based structures. The fields usually adopt the structure of the source table's fields. The field's properties can indicate the following:

▶ Whether the field is a key figure or characteristic

▶ If the field is a key figure, the aggregation behavior of the key figure

▶ Authorization relevance of the field

Open ODS view restriction

 Open ODS view can be used to indicate if a field contains a key figure or a characteristic, but it cannot be used to define hierarchies. As an SAP BW system uses a BW-specific internal format to specify a hierarchy structure, it is not possible to use an Open ODS view to identify a hierarchy.

A field can be associated with either an InfoObject or another Open ODS view. If a field is associated with another InfoObject, it can inherit all the attributes and text for that InfoObject. Similarly, if a field is associated with another Open ODS view, it can utilize the data of that other Open ODS view to enrich itself.

Once the Open ODS view is created, queries can be created to enable reporting.

An Open ODS view can accept data from four different types of sources.

2.1.1   Sources for Open ODS views

▶ Datasources (BW)—A datasource on a table helps expose an external table in a database to SAP BW's Open ODS view. Datasources can be created via RSO2. If data needs to be extracted from a table, expose the table via a datasource. Some of the supported source system types are BW, SAP, ODP extraction technique, and DBCONNECT.

▶ Database table or view—Data in tables or views in any schema within SAP HANA can be viewed using this option.

▶ Advanced Data Store Object (aDSO)—Usually aDSOs can be exposed directly to SAP BW queries. The advantage of having an aDSO as a source to Open ODS views is to use a transaction datasource as master data or the other way around. All reporting takes place using the active table of the Advanced DSO.

▶ Transformation—A source table is usually interfaced directly to an Open ODS view, but in some situations, it might be required that some fields undergo some transformations before being exposed to the Open ODS view. In that case, it might be required that the source for an Open ODS view be a transformation attached to the datasource.

Open ODS view availability

Open ODS view is available only on SAP BW systems running on SAP HANA databases.

2.1.2   Transporting Open ODS views

Transports for Open ODS view uses SAP's TLOGO framework. The objects are transportable and the transportable object type is either FBPA or FBPD (SAP-delivered object). In order to transport the Open ODS view, all dependent objects should be available in the target system. If the Open ODS view is created on a source table, that source table and its datasource should reside in the target system. The Open ODS view does not hold the connection information. The view is connected to the source system and the RSLOGSYSMAP table in the target system usually holds the source-to-target-system mapping details so that the transport can correctly recognize the target system and the table to which the Open ODS view is connected.

2.1.3 Advantages and disadvantages of Open ODS views

Advantages

1. Open ODS view is a view on the source table structures, so it does not persist data

2. Instead of using InfoObjects, Open ODS view utilizes field-based constructs. This helps a developer to quickly implement queries and do a quicker proof of concept.

3. Open ODS view can connect a field's definition to either an InfoObject or another Open ODS view. This enables a field to utilize an existing BW definition to enrich queries.

Disadvantage

1. Open ODS view should be created on smaller-sized source tables. Query performance gets degraded if the source table size is big.

2.1.4 An example utilizing Open ODS views

The next example shows how to do a quick proof of concept for an Open ODS view. The example utilizes the source system to be a datasource (BW). Custom zzcus_reg table has been created in SAP. It stores CUSTOMER ID, CUSTOMER STATE, and CUSTOMER REGION. Create an Open ODS view on this table and expose it to create a query on the basic table without creating InfoObjects.

1. Display the zzcus_reg Table—In order to display the zzcus_reg table, use the SE16 transaction code (TCODE), as shown in Figure 2.1.

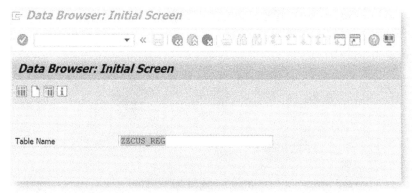

Figure 2.1: Table name being displayed via SE16

2. When the data browser screen displays, click the NUMBER OF EN-TRIES button and check how many rows are available. In this example, there are 12 rows in the table as shown in Figure 2.2.

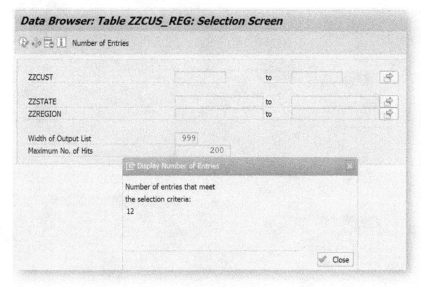

Figure 2.2: Display number of entries in a table

3. Execute the TCODE RSO2 and create a datasource on the table zzcus_reg. In this example, the datasource name is ZZCUS_REG_ATTR as shown in Figure 2.3.

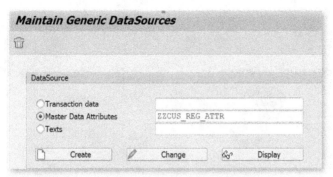

Figure 2.3: Name of the datasource to be created

4.   Once the CREATE button is clicked, a new screen, as shown in Figure 2.4 opens.

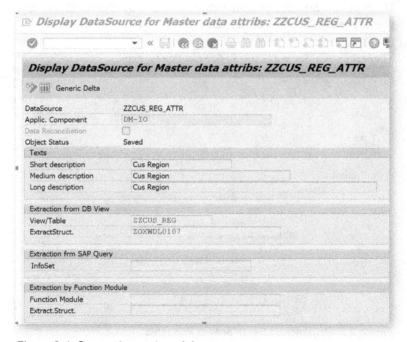

Figure 2.4: Screen to create a datasource

5.   After filling in the details shown on the screen, click SAVE. A new window appears, see Figure 2.5.

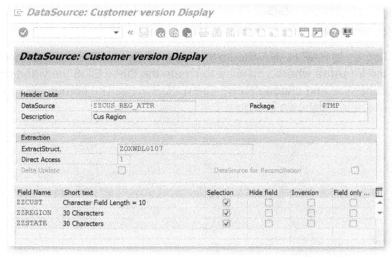

Figure 2.5: Choose the fields that are needed to pass filter values to the datasource

6. Once you click SAVE, your datasource is created! To cross-check if the datasource is working properly, go to TCODE RSA3, put the datasource name for master data attributes and click EXTRACTION, as shown in Figure 2.6.

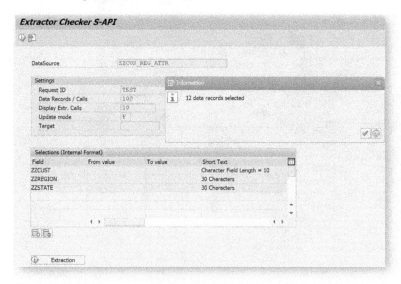

Figure 2.6: Datasource extractor checker

In our example, the datasource extracts the same number of rows as the zzcus_reg table.

7. Log on to SAP HANA Studio to create an Open ODS view. Choose the InfoArea where you want to create the Open ODS view and then right-click and choose NEW • OPEN ODS VIEW. The screen will look like what is shown in Figure 2.7.

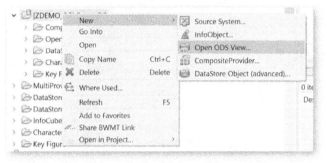

Figure 2.7: Menu option to create an Open ODS view

8. The screen shown in Figure 2.8 pops up. Click NEXT.

Figure 2.8: Name the Open ODS view

9. Select the datasource that you have created to attach to the Open ODS view. For our example, it is zzcus_reg_attr. Choose the highlighted datasource, as shown in Figure 2.9, and click FINISH.

Figure 2.9: Choose datasource for the Open ODS view

10. Click the MASTER DATA tab. Fix the headings of the fields, if needed. Click ▮ to activate the Open ODS view. If you want to see data flowing through the Open ODS view, go to the SAP BW admin workbench and enter TCODE RSA1. Find the Open ODS view object ZOODSVW, right-click on the object, and click DISPLAY DATA. A snapshot of the data visible via the Open ODS view is shown in Figure 2.10.

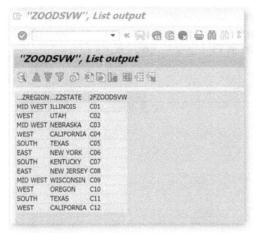

Figure 2.10: Data display via Open ODS views

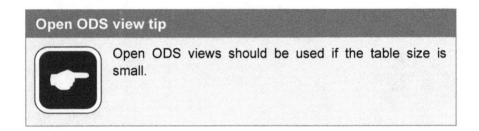

2.2 Composite providers

Before SAP HANA was introduced, it was possible to combine data in SAP BW by either using multiproviders or InfoSets. Similar to Open ODS views, multiproviders, InfoSets, and composite providers are views on top of underlying InfoProviders. None of these objects store data; they are all views. Multiproviders allow joining tables together using a method called *union*. InfoSets, on the other hand, allows joining objects by using database joins such as left- or right-outer join. As InfoSets contain database join conditions, queries on InfoSets are considerably slower in querying the database. SAP has a new type of provider on SAP HANA where it is possible to do a union, inner, left- or right-outer join. This new type of provider is called SAP HANA Composite Provider (HCP) and is meant to replace all the old objects such as multiproviders, old composite providers, InfoSets, and transient providers. The other objects will not be phased out, but SAP HCP is now the recommended object to be used for all reporting in SAP BW on SAP HANA where objects need to be combined for reporting purposes.

InfoSet usage

You still need to consider using InfoSets, if you want to use a key date for the join condition. Composite providers do not yet provide that feature.

2.2.1   Supported providers within composite providers

Before creating composite providers, decide what sort of link to use between different source, or part, providers.

If composite providers are created with links between objects of the type *union*, you can only use the following source providers: InfoCubes, DSOs (classic and advanced), semantically partitioned objects, Open ODS views, virtual providers, InfoObjects, InfoSets, and aggregation levels.

If links are type *join*, then you can only use InfoCubes, DSOs, semantically partitioned objects (one per composite provider), and InfoObjects.

If both *union* and *join* are needed in a composite provider, you can only use InfoCubes, DSOs, and InfoObjects.

2.2.2   Inner join and outer join details

Inner joins return rows when there is at least one row from both tables that matches the join condition. Inner joins eliminate the rows that do not have a match.

Outer joins, however, return all rows from at least one of the tables or views mentioned in the FROM clause, as long as those rows meet any

WHERE condition. All rows are retrieved from the left table referenced with a left-outer join, and all rows from the right table referenced in a right-outer join.

2.2.3 Scenarios within a composite provider

Composite providers can be a combination of various joins within joins/unions. Some possible combinations of joins include:

▶ Inner join within left-outer join, see Figure 2.11.

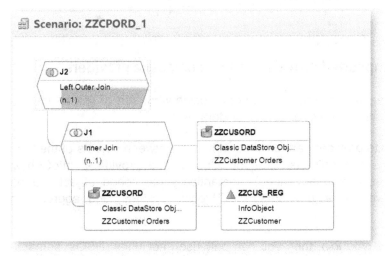

Figure 2.11: Inner join within left-outer join

The system will first evaluate the INNER JOIN, J1. The system then joins that to table ZZCUSORD via a LEFT-OUTER JOIN, J2. The left-outer table is the result of the join J1.

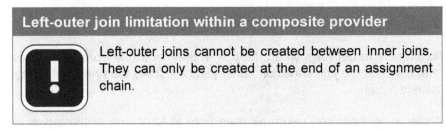

Left-outer join limitation within a composite provider

Left-outer joins cannot be created between inner joins. They can only be created at the end of an assignment chain.

▶ Union within a *join operation*—As shown in Figure 2.12, the system first evaluates the UNION U1. U1 is the union of two objects called ZZCUSORD and ZZCUORD1. After the UNION U1 object is evaluated, the system then performs a left-outer join between U1 and InfoObject ZZCUS_REG.

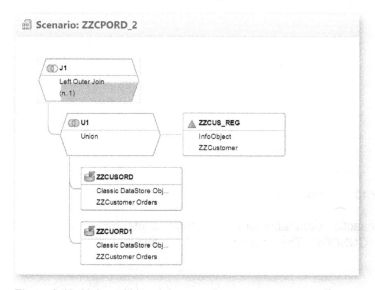

Figure 2.12: Union within a join operation

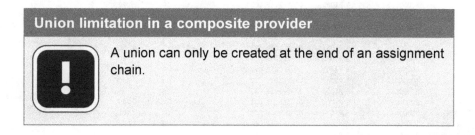

Union limitation in a composite provider

A union can only be created at the end of an assignment chain.

2.2.4   An example utilizing composite provider

The next example shows how a composite provider can join a transaction table to a master data table by using a left-outer join. You will store customer region master data in the InfoObject ZZCUS_REG. The customer order transaction data will be stored in a classic DSO. Composite provider will be used to join these two objects to show customer orders with additional master data.

11. Master data used in this example will be customer region table: zzcus_reg. This is stored in an InfoObject called ZZCUS_REG. The content of this object is shown in Figure 2.13.

Customer ID	Customer State	Region
C01	Illinois	Mid West
C02	Utah	West
C03	Nebraska	Mid West
C04	California	West
C05	Texas	South
C06	New York	East
C07	Kentucky	South
C08	New Jersey	East
C09	Wisconsin	Mid West
C10	Oregon	West
C11	Texas	South
C12	California	West

Figure 2.13: Customer region

12. The transaction data table for this example is attached to classic DSO ZZCUSORD. The data for this DSO is shown in Figure 2.14.

Order Nu	Order Ite	Product	Order Da	Customer	Order Qty	Order Valı
30000001	1	P1001	01.01.2016	C01	15	239.85
30000002	1	P1001	01.02.2016	C02	20	319.8
30000003	1	P1001	01.03.2016	C03	100	1599
30000003	2	P1002	01.04.2016	C04	2	60
30000003	3	P1003	01.05.2016	C05	10	70
30000003	4	P1004	01.06.2016	C06	20	240
30000007	1	P1005	01.07.2016	C07	30	389.7
30000008	1	P1004	01.01.2016	C08	1	12
30000008	2	P1001	01.02.2016	C09	2	31.98
30000008	3	P1002	01.03.2016	C10	3	90
30000008	4	P1001	01.04.2016	C11	4	63.96
30000012	1	P1002	01.05.2016	C12	5	150
30000013	1	P1003	01.06.2016	C01	15	105
30000014	1	P1004	01.07.2016	C02	20	240
30000015	1	P1004	01.01.2016	C03	100	1200
30000016	1	P1001	01.02.2016	C04	2	31.98
30000017	1	P1002	01.03.2016	C05	10	300
30000018	1	P1003	01.04.2016	C06	20	140
30000019	1	P1002	01.01.2016	C07	30	900
30000020	1	P1003	01.02.2016	C08	1	7
30000021	1	P1004	01.03.2016	C09	2	24
30000022	1	P1002	01.04.2016	C10	3	90
30000023	1	P1003	01.05.2016	C11	4	28
30000024	1	P1004	01.06.2016	C12	5	60

Figure 2.14: Customer orders

13. Create a composite provider that joins the two tables, shown in Figure 2.13 and Figure 2.14, to show customer region alongside the key figures ORDER QTY and ORDER VALUE.

14. Listed in Figure 2.15 are all the objects that are used to create the composite provider.

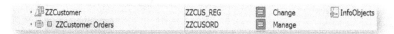

Figure 2.15: Objects being used to create composite provider

15. Log on to SAP HANA Studio, go to the chosen InfoArea, right-click on the applicable InfoArea, and then click NEW • COMPOSITE PROVIDER. This is shown in Figure 2.16.

Figure 2.16: Menu option to create new composite provider

16. On the next screen (shown in Figure 2.17), give the name of the composite provider and its description. I have chosen to name the composite provider ZZCPORD. Click NEXT.

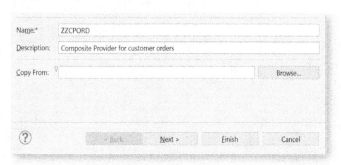

Figure 2.17: Create composite provider screen, continued

17. Next, decide on the type of link needed to connect the part providers. ZZCUS_REG is the provider for master data and ZZCUSORD is the provider for transaction data. Add the two part providers via the ADD button, as shown in Figure 2.18. Click FINISH.

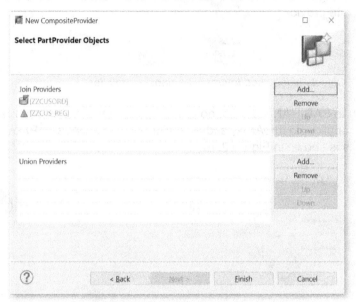

Figure 2.18: Create composite provider screen, continued

18. On the screen that opens, go to the SCENARIO tab, as shown in Figure 2.19. In this tab, you need to declare the target fields and map the source fields to the target fields.

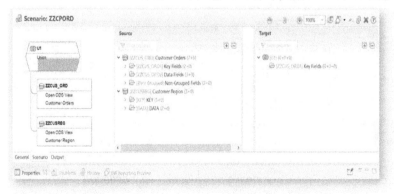

Figure 2.19: Map source fields to target fields in the composite provider

19. In Figure 2.20, J1 shows that the join type chosen for the linkage of two part providers is left-outer join. CUSTOMER ORDERS DSO is the primary join participant, with the customer master data object being secondary in the join condition (left-outer join). The join condition equates CUSTOMER ID fields from both source tables. Select all fields from both source tables on the left-hand side and drop them into the target composite provider to the extreme right-hand side, as shown in Figure 2.20. Then map the CUSTOMER ID field from both source tables to the target table. This completes the creation of the composite provider!

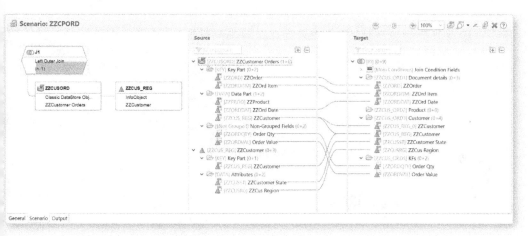

Figure 2.20: Explanation for the join conditions

20. To preview the data that will flow through the newly created composite provider, you can go to the SAP BW back-end system and then type in TCODE RSA1. In RSA1, find the composite provider, right-click on the provider, and then click DISPLAY DATA, as shown in Figure 2.21.

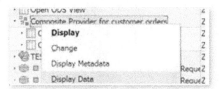

Figure 2.21: Context menu for composite provider via RSA1

21. Figure 2.22 shows the data that gets displayed when you choose the DISPLAY DATA context menu. The last two columns flow from the

master data InfoObject, whereas the first eight columns flow in from the transaction data table.

"ZZCPORD", List output

InfoProvider	ZZOrder	ZZOrd Date	ZZOrd Item	ZZCustomer	ZZCustomer	ZZORDQTY	Order Value	ZZCustomer State	ZZCus Region
ZZCUSORD	0030000013	01.06.2016	000001	C01	C01	15.000	105.000	ILLINOIS	MID WEST
ZZCUSORD	0030000008	01.04.2016	000004	C11	C11	4.000	63.960	TEXAS	SOUTH
ZZCUSORD	0030000003	01.05.2016	000003	C05	C05	10.000	70.000	TEXAS	SOUTH
ZZCUSORD	0030000001	01.01.2016	000001	C01	C01	15.000	239.850	ILLINOIS	MID WEST
ZZCUSORD	0030000008	01.03.2016	000003	C10	C10	3.000	90.000	OREGON	WEST
ZZCUSORD	0030000019	01.01.2016	000001	C07	C07	30.000	900.000	KENTUCKY	SOUTH
ZZCUSORD	0030000008	01.02.2016	000002	C09	C09	2.000	31.980	WISCONSIN	MID WEST
ZZCUSORD	0030000016	01.02.2016	000001	C04	C04	2.000	31.980	CALIFORNIA	WEST
ZZCUSORD	0030000020	01.02.2016	000001	C08	C08	1.000	7.000	NEW JERSEY	EAST
ZZCUSORD	0030000014	01.07.2016	000001	C02	C02	20.000	240.000	UTAH	WEST
ZZCUSORD	0030000021	01.03.2016	000001	C09	C09	2.000	24.000	WISCONSIN	MID WEST
ZZCUSORD	0030000023	01.05.2016	000001	C11	C11	4.000	28.000	TEXAS	SOUTH
ZZCUSORD	0030000022	01.04.2016	000001	C10	C10	3.000	90.000	OREGON	WEST
ZZCUSORD	0030000003	01.04.2016	000002	C04	C04	2.000	60.000	CALIFORNIA	WEST
ZZCUSORD	0030000008	01.01.2016	000001	C08	C08	1.000	12.000	NEW JERSEY	EAST
ZZCUSORD	0030000003	01.03.2016	000001	C03	C03	100.000	1,599.000	NEBRASKA	MID WEST
ZZCUSORD	0030000018	01.04.2016	000001	C06	C06	20.000	140.000	NEW YORK	EAST
ZZCUSORD	0030000007	01.07.2016	000001	C07	C07	30.000	389.700	KENTUCKY	SOUTH
ZZCUSORD	0030000002	01.02.2016	000001	C02	C02	20.000	319.800	UTAH	WEST
ZZCUSORD	0030000003	01.06.2016	000004	C06	C06	20.000	240.000	NEW YORK	EAST
ZZCUSORD	0030000012	01.05.2016	000001	C12	C12	5.000	150.000	CALIFORNIA	WEST
ZZCUSORD	0030000015	01.01.2016	000001	C03	C03	100.000	1,200.000	NEBRASKA	MID WEST
ZZCUSORD	0030000017	01.03.2016	000001	C05	C05	10.000	300.000	TEXAS	SOUTH
ZZCUSORD	0030000024	01.06.2016	000001	C12	C12	5.000	60.000	CALIFORNIA	WEST

Figure 2.22: Data displayed via composite provider

2.3 Advanced DSOs

The Advanced DSO is supposed to become the sole object to replace all other types of providers such as InfoCubes, DSOs (classic and write-optimized), and InfoSets. These objects can be used if you have SAP BW 7.4, SPS 8.0, SAP HANA version 1.0 revision 83, or higher. More about this object will be discussed in subsequent chapters.

3 Modeling with SAP HANA Studio

If you are using an SAP HANA database, data modeling can now be done using the SAP HANA Studio available via the eclipse-based integrated development environment (IDE). With the introduction of the SAP HANA database, fewer object types than the amount for traditional relational databases are needed. In SAP HANA, you can do all of the data modeling with the following four objects: composite providers, Advanced DSOs, Open ODS views, and InfoObjects. SAP HANA-based metadata objects can now be easily created using SAP HANA Studio. The SAP HANA-based objects need a powerful user interface in order to visualize the metadata. The eclipse-based tool was introduced because of the increasing complexity of objects, to provide a flexible reporting environment for creating the complex objects. These complex objects cannot be created in the SAP BW administrator workbench (via RSA1).

If you want to work with SAP HANA Studio and SAP BW data modeling, you need to download it from the SAP Service marketplace (http://service.sap.com/installnw74 ⇨ Installation ⇨ Clients). SAP HANA Studio needs to be installed with the "BW Perspective". This perspective contains all tools that are needed to create BW models.

3.1 SAP BW modeling perspective

The SAP BW modeling perspective provides two tools: editor and view. Editor is used to edit the BW metadata object. This section of SAP HANA Studio is identified by G in Figure 3.1. The view is further subdivided into five views as shown in Figure 3.1.

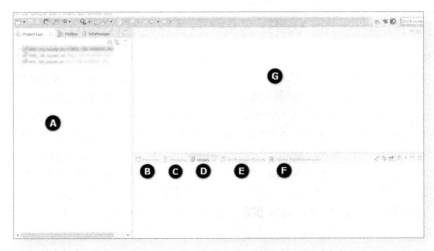

Figure 3.1: SAP BW perspective in SAP HANA Studio

3.1.1 Project view

Project view is where you can set up connectivity to an SAP BW database. In Figure 3.1, this area is identified by the A. On the project workspace screen, right-click • NEW • PROJECT. This is shown in Figure 3.2.

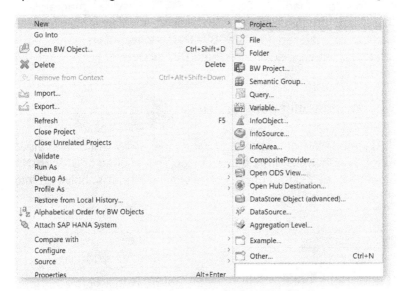

Figure 3.2: Create a new project using SAP HANA Studio

The next screen shows all the database connections that have been set up via SAP Logon Pad. Choose the connection for your SAP BW system. (If you have not set up the SAP BW connection, use SAP Logon Pad to do so and then come back into SAP HANA Studio to set up a project.)

Once you create a project, double-click on the project name. The system will prompt you for the UserID/password details. Once that is entered, you will gain access to the three subfolders in the project view, as shown in Figure 3.3.

Figure 3.3: Subfolders in the project view

► FAVORITES—When you edit an SAP BW object, you can mark that object as a favorite. All favorite objects appear in this folder.

► BW REPOSITORY is a folder that shows all the SAP BW objects according to InfoArea. Under the InfoArea, the objects are divided according to the object type, as shown in Figure 3.4.

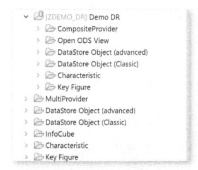

Figure 3.4: Object types under InfoArea

► DATASOURCES—This is a list of all datasources available to be used in the SAP BW system. The list is shown by source system.

3.1.2 Properties view

When you are editing an object in editor view, the properties of that object are displayed in the properties view page (identified by B in Figure 3.1). Properties include PACKAGE, APPLICATION COMPONENT, PERSON RESPONSIBLE, ACTIVE STATE, VERSION STATE, CREATED ON, LAST CHANGED BY, LAST CHANGED ON, ORIGINAL LANGUAGE, and ORIGINAL SYSTEM. The properties view screen for the shipment header datasource is shown in Figure 3.5.

Figure 3.5: Properties view

3.1.3 Problems view

While editing an SAP BW object using the editor screen, if there are any problems encountered during activation of the object, that problem is displayed in a new view (identified by C in Figure 3.1).

3.1.4 History view

History view (identified by D in Figure 3.1) shows the various versions for that SAP BW object, together with the version type and creation date.

3.1.5 SAP BW reporting preview

While editing the object, if you want to see data for that object, click the pane called BW REPORTING PREVIEW (identified by E in Figure 3.1). You need to click the REFRESH DATA PREVIEW button to populate data in this preview screen.

3.1.6 Master data maintenance

This view will give you the flexibility to maintain master data. This view is identified by E in Figure 3.1.

4   What is an Advanced DSO?

Since SAP BW V1.2B, multiprovider has been the only reporting so-lution. A multiprovider is a union of different SAP BW objects. It does not contain any data, but is a view that combines data from different data providers such as InfoCubes, InfoSets, classic datas-tore objects (DSOs), and a variety of other objects. When SAP re-leased SAP NW BW 7.4 SP8 (recommendation is to wait till SP9), the Advanced DSO became the central data modeling object in SAP BW. Currently, this object, along with the new composite provider and Open ODS view, will replace all the multiproviders, classic DSOs, and InfoSets in SAP BW. These old objects will continue to exist for downward compatibility, but these three objects will now be the combined primary objects to create reporting solutions.

So, what is an *Advanced DSO (aDSO)*? An aDSO is an SAP BW object that combines the functionality of both InfoCubes and classic DSOs. It is used for both storage of data (like a classic DSO) and reporting function-alities (like InfoCube). According to SAP, aDSOs are now the center of data modeling as they provide features such as:

- ► Simplified data modeling technique
    - ► They can be used for both data persistency and reporting
    - ► They use both InfoObject and field-based modeling
- ► Faster activation
- ► Faster data load timing (as they are based on an enhanced re-quest management system), when compared to a classic DSO
- ► Faster querying time, when compared to a classic DSO

Advanced DSO objects can be created by using the SAP HANA eclipse modeling tool. Creation through the RSA1 modeling workbench is not allowed.

aDSO technical name length

Similar to a classic DSO, the length of the technical name of an aDSO cannot exceed nine characters.

4.1   Advanced DSO tables

The back-end database design of an Advanced DSO object is still the same as the classic DSO. In spite of the back-end design being similar to a classic DSO, the flexibility that an aDSO provides for modeling is much higher than a classic DSO. Like the classic DSO, an aDSO is made up of three core database tables, as shown in the diagram in Figure 4.1.

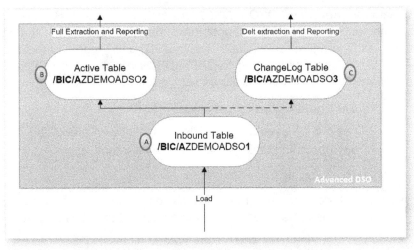

Figure 4.1: Back-end tables that form an Advanced DSO

▶   INBOUND TABLE—The inbound table is identified by A in Figure 4.1. This table is similar to the "new" table that loads data into the classic DSO. Data gets extracted via the InfoPackage/DTP and gets loaded into the inbound table.

▶ CHANGELOG TABLE—If delta changes need to be pushed further to datatargets, then the activation program pushes the delta data to the changelog table. If there are no datatargets to feed, the changelog table can be left blank. This is slightly different from how the classic DSO functionality works. For classic DSOs, the changelog table will always be filled in.

▶ ACTIVE TABLE—An active table is where data resides for reporting purposes. In some instances (in SAP BW 7.4 and onwards), data from an active table can be combined with data from an inbound table for reporting.

4.2 Modeling properties

Modeling properties can be accessed in SAP HANA Studio by choosing the option to create a new aDSO. The system prompts for the technical name of the aDSO and then shows the screen to choose the aDSO modeling properties. The way the system uses the three core tables (Inbound/Activation/Change log) depends upon the way an aDSO is designed using SAP HANA Studio via the modeling properties. A sample modeling properties screen for an aDSO is shown in Figure 4.2.

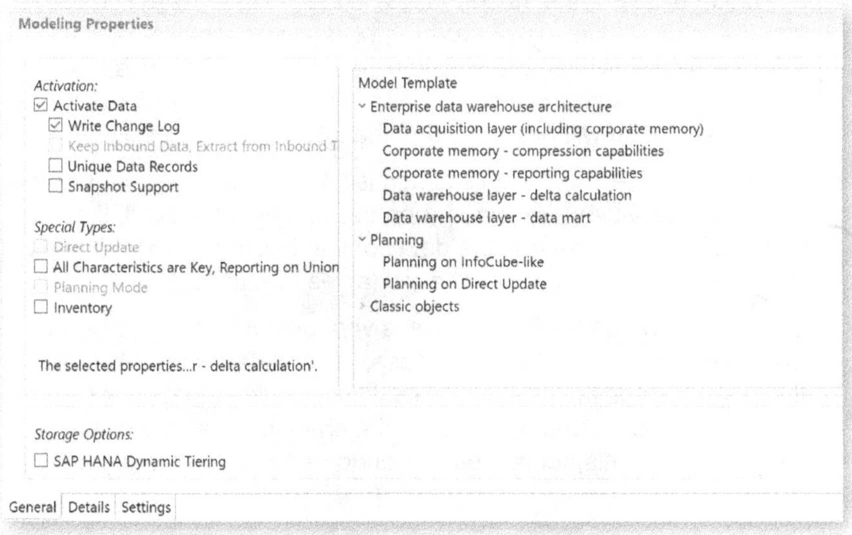

Figure 4.2: Modeling properties for an aDSO

The behavior of the aDSO and the usage of the three tables will be determined by the options selected in the ACTIVATION and SPECIAL TYPES sections, as shown in Figure 4.2 (left-hand side of the screen).

4.2.1 Activation section

ACTIVATE DATA—Data is usually loaded into the inbound table (except for the aDSO of the type DIRECT UPDATE). When this box is checked, data will be pushed from the inbound table into the active table once the activation process starts. Along with activation, four different activities may or may not happen.

1. WRITE CHANGE LOG—When this box is checked, data is also written to the changelog table once the activation process starts. If an aDSO is required to feed to other datatargets, then a changelog table is usually used to create delta updates to the target. The activation process involves comparing inbound data with the active table. Based on that, it creates deltas and stores them in the changelog table. Once the target is ready to receive the delta data, the changelog delta records are pushed into the target.

2. KEEP INBOUND DATA, EXTRACT FROM INBOUND TABLE—Usually, in the activation process, the inbound table is loaded into the active table, and the inbound table is cleared. The changelog table is used to feed the targets. When the checkbox is switched on for this option, it means that the inbound table will need to retain data, and extraction to the next target will happen using the inbound table.

3. UNIQUE DATA RECORDS—This option is usually checked to save time during the activation process. When this option is checked, the activation process knows that the data coming in is unique and it does not compare the active and inbound tables for duplicates.

4. SNAPSHOT SUPPORT—This feature is very useful for the datasources that do not support delta. In this case, when a data load takes place, the system reads the inbound table, finds the delta that needs to be reversed out and creates entries in the changelog table with the reversed image. This helps create pseudo-deltas for the target objects.

4.2.2 Special types section

1. DIRECT UPDATE—This option is usually used to bypass the inbound table or changelog table and write data directly to the active table. The data is written to the active table either via DTP or an API.

2. ALL CHARACTERISTICS ARE KEY, REPORTING ON UNION OF INBOUND AND ACTIVE TABLE—As the heading suggests, in this option, the active table has all the characteristics as the key. This is similar to the standard InfoCube design where all characters were considered to be keys. The inbound table can be considered to be the F table and the active table can be compared with the E table, where data resides in a standard cube after compression. Similar to how reporting on a cube involves combining data from both E and F tables, the reporting on this option also combines data from the active table and the inbound table for completeness.

3. PLANNING MODE—This type of aDSO is used for planning. (The planning DSO is not discussed in this book.)

4. INVENTORY—This type of aDSO is used to store non-cumulative or inventory-type data.

On the right-hand side of the modeling properties screen, shown in Figure 4.2, the user needs to choose a default data model for the aDSO. The user can either choose from the left-hand side (ACTIVATION/SPECIAL TYPE) or the right-hand side of the screen (MODEL TEMPLATE). The result will be the same. As soon as the user chooses a model template, the ACTIVATION checkboxes and SPECIAL TYPES checkboxes get enabled based on the model chosen. The model template and the activation and special types sections are related and defined in the table. Table 4.1 discusses core EDW components; it does not cover planning objects.

Option #	Model Template	Activation	Special Types	Comment
1	Data acquisition layer (incl. corporate memory)	All unchecked	All unchecked	This type of model gives the capability of creating a data storage table like a PSA or a write-optimized DSO.
2	Corporate memory— compression capabilities	Checked— 1) Activate Data	All unchecked	This type of model utilizes the inbound layer to load the data. But for better storage options that utilize less space, it is then loaded into the active table. The active table requires that the data is compressed per the semantic key and that data is not stored according to the technical key (inbound layer). When the data is loaded to the active table, the inbound table is cleared.
3	Corporate memory – reporting capabilities	Checked— 2) Activate Data 2) Keep Inbound Data, Extract from Inbound Table	All unchecked	This type of model is the same as corporate memory—compression capabilities. The only difference is that when data is loaded to the active table, the Inbound table is NOT cleared.
4	Data warehouse layer—delta calculation	Checked— 1) Activate Data 2) Write changelog 3) Unique Data Records (Optional)	Unchecked	This setting corresponds to the classic DSO.
5	Data warehouse layer—datamart	Checked— 1) Activate Data	All Characteristics are key, reporting on the union of the inbound and active tables	This is the standard InfoCube setting.

Table 4.1: Model template for aDSOs

SAP has provided five distinct template models to create Advanced DSOs for core data warehousing needs. Depending upon the data model, one can choose the template so that the system will automatically choose the modeling properties that correspond to that template model. If you are comfortable using the modeling properties, you should go ahead and use them. On the other hand, if you know the requirements for which you need to create the aDSO (loading, staging, or reporting layer), you should use the model template instead, and let the system choose the modeling properties automatically. Each modeling option is described in detail in the upcoming sections with an example of how to create and use that particular aDSO. The templates that are described in the next five chapters are for the core data warehousing needs. (The planning DSOs are not described.)

5 Model template—data acquisition layer—including corporate memory

The term, data acquisition, means that the Advanced DSO will be used to acquire data from the source system. This model is the first layer (loading layer) into which data will get extracted. It has the modeling properties shown in Figure 5.1.

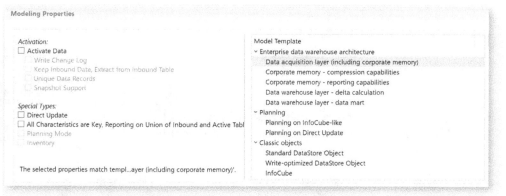

Figure 5.1: Data acquisition layer (including corporate memory)

When a user chooses this model template, all boxes under modeling properties are unchecked. If the box against ACTIVATE is unchecked, it means that the data does not get loaded to the active table. The check-box beside CHANGE LOG is unchecked, which means further loading into datatargets does not happen using the changelog. In summary, this means that the inbound table is used to load data into SAP BW. Also, the target will receive its data from the inbound table. You might choose to utilize this option to create a corporate memory layer, which would remain the single source of truth for that dataset. Data could be extracted from this layer and pushed into multiple datatargets for cleansing. This will be the historical source of truth.

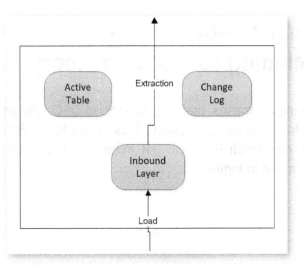

Figure 5.2: Database table usage for the data acquisition layer (including corporate memory) model

Figure 5.2 depicts the inbound table being utilized to load data into, and to feed data to, other targets. This type of model looks exactly like the PSA or the write-optimized classic DSO.

This type of Advanced DSO is also called a corporate memory layer. Data stored in this layer is untransformed and raw. Once data is collected in this layer, it can be fed into targets where data can be further transformed. As data is in its original format, creating reports is not recommended in this layer, as the key is a technical key (request number, data packet number, and record number). Reporting will be slower compared to reports created on the active table, where data is already aggregated for better reporting capability. This layer accepts data at a field level or at an InfoObject level. Hence, it is extremely easy to model this type of aDSO.

5.1.1 Functionality

► Only one table is used. The inbound table is used to load data in the warehouse and also feed other datatargets.

► As there is only one table involved, loading is faster than any other model.

► Although the system does not use the active table or changelog table, it still creates them so that system adjustments can be done easily at a later point in time, if the usage of the aDSO changes.

► It is like a write-optimized DSO.

► The system generates a unique technical key made up of request number, datapacket ID, and record ID.

► Reporting should not be done on this object as the data is stored at the technical-key level and not the semantic-key level.

5.1.2 Recommended use of this model

► This model should be used for faster data loading time.

► This model should be used when data is being loaded for the first time into the business warehouse system. It is useful to utilize this type of aDSO in the loading layer.

► This layer can handle a large load volume because it consists of only one table.

► This model should be used to store historical data.

5.1.3 How to create an aDSO of the type—data acquisition layer—including corporate memory aDSO

This section will show how an aDSO of this model template can be created in SAP BW using SAP HANA Studio.

1. Log on to SAP HANA Studio with your SAP BW credentials and go to the InfoArea where you want to create the aDSO.

2. Right-click on the InfoArea and then select NEW • DATASTORE OBJECT (ADVANCED), as shown in Figure 5.3.

Figure 5.3: Step to create a new aDSO

3. After you choose the option to create an aDSO, the following screen, as shown in Figure 5.4, pops up to get the technical name of the aDSO.

Figure 5.4: Create a new Advanced Data Store Object

4. Enter the technical name for the aDSO. In this exercise, the name of the aDSO is chosen as ZADSO_1. After naming the aDSO, click FIN-ISH.

5. The next screen displayed asks for the modeling properties (on the left-hand side) or the template model (on the right-hand side). By default, the boxes for ACTIVATE DATA and WRITE CHANGE LOG are checked, as shown in Figure 5.5.

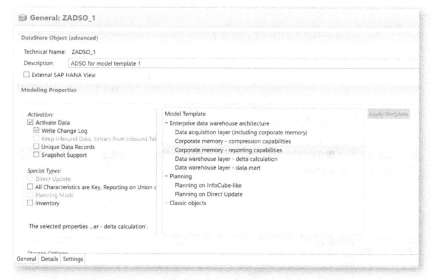

Figure 5.5: Default modeling properties chosen by the system

6. Click on the first template model, DATA ACQUISITION LAYER (INCLUDING CORPORATE MEMORY) • APPLY TEMPLATE.

7. Once the template is applied, the checkboxes for ACTIVATE DATA and WRITE CHANGE LOG disappear (as shown in Figure 5.6). This is because only the inbound table needs to be loaded and no activation is needed. Also, all datatargets need to be loaded using the inbound table. Although the changelog table gets created in this data model, it is not used by the system. It remains empty.

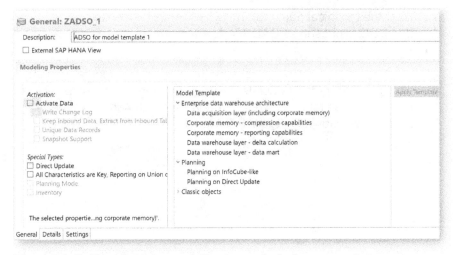

Figure 5.6: Settings for data acquisition layer—including corporate memory

8. Once the template model is set, go to the DETAILS tab. The initial screen is shown in Figure 5.7.

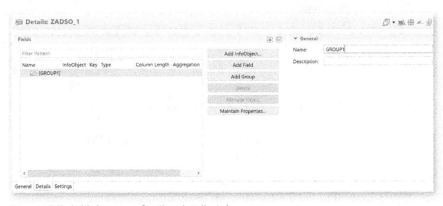

Figure 5.7: Initial screen for the details tab

9. Click the ADD FIELD button. Fill in the field information, as shown in Table 5.1.

Field	Data Type	Length
Order Num	NUMC	10
Order Item	NUMC	4
Product ID	NUMC	18
Order Date	DATE	8
Customer ID	NUMC	10
Order Qty	Decimal	17,2
Order Value	Decimal	17,2

Table 5.1: Fields in an aDSO

Seven fields need to be created. The final screen for fields is shown in Figure 5.8. Note that the MANAGE KEYS button is greyed out as the inbound layer has technical keys instead of semantic keys.

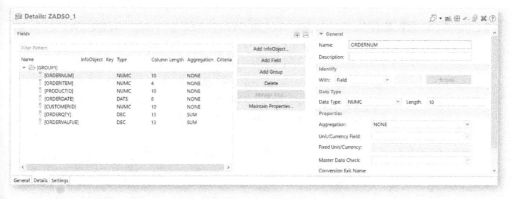

Figure 5.8: Details tab for an aDSO

10. Click [Ctrl] + [F3] or the ACTIVATE button (⬛) on the top menu bar.

11. The aDSO object has now been activated.

12. To analyze how the active, inbound, and changelog tables are being used at the database level, create a flatfile transformation to the aDSO and load a .CSV file into the aDSO. Locate the InfoArea and aDSO ZADSO_1 in RSA1 and create a new transformation with the source as a flatfile datasource and the target as the aDSO. Load the flatfile into the aDSO. (This step is not covered in detail, as this is a regular SAP BW step and is not a new feature.)

13. Once the data gets loaded, log on to the SAP BW administrator workbench and go to TCODE *SE16*. Search for the table *ZADSO_1*. Five tables get listed, as shown in Figure 5.9.

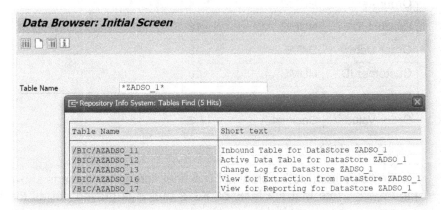

Figure 5.9: Database tables associated with the aDSO

14. Although only the inbound table is being used, the system creates the active and changelog tables, but they remain unused. The other two tables are views that the system creates for its own usage.

15. A data snapshot for the inbound table shows that the first three fields are technical keys, as shown in Figure 5.10. The technical keys are request number, datapacket ID, and data record ID.

Data Browser: Table /BIC/AZADSO_11 Select Entries   25

Request Transaction Sequence Number	DataPacket	Data record	R	ORDERNUM	ORDERITEM	PRODUCTID	CUSTOMERID	ORDERQTY
20171221042837000001000	000001	1		0000000001	0100	0001012016	0000000015	239.85
20171221042837000001000	000001	2		0000000001	0100	0001022016	0000000020	319.80
20171221042837000001000	000001	3		0000000001	0100	0001032016	0000000100	1,599.00
20171221042837000001000	000001	4		0000000002	0100	0001042016	0000000002	60.00
20171221042837000001000	000001	5		0000000003	0100	0001052016	0000000010	70.00
20171221042837000001000	000001	6		0000000004	0100	0001062016	0000000020	240.00
20171221042837000001000	000001	7		0000000001	0100	0001072016	0000000030	389.70

Figure 5.10: Data content for the inbound database table

16. The active and changelog tables are empty, as shown in Figure 5.11 and Figure 5.12.

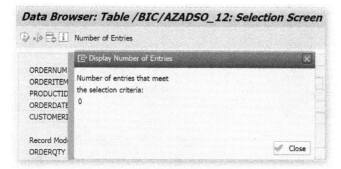

Figure 5.11: Active table is empty

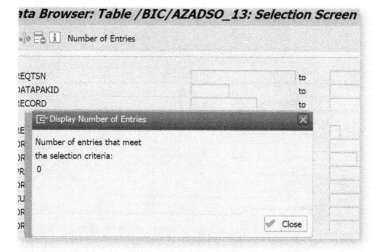

Figure 5.12: Change log table is empty

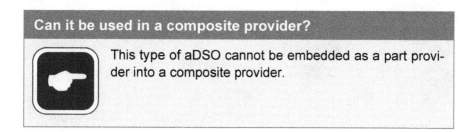

Can it be used in a composite provider?

This type of aDSO cannot be embedded as a part provider into a composite provider.

6 Model template—corporate memory—compression capabilities

The second template model that SAP has provided, corporate memory—compression capabilities, also deals with the inbound, or loading, layer. It has the modeling properties as shown in Figure 6.1.

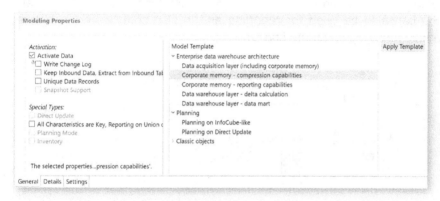

Figure 6.1: Corporate memory—compression capabilities

When a user chooses this model template, all boxes under modeling properties are unchecked except for ACTIVATE DATA, meaning that the data gets loaded into the active table. The box for WRITE CHANGE LOG is unchecked, which means further loading into datatargets does not happen using the changelog. In summary:

▶ The inbound table is used to load data into SAP BW.

▶ When the activation process is kicked off, the data from the inbound table is then loaded into the active table.

▶ As the data in the active table is based on the semantic key, data is compressed (activated) per the key.

▶ The target tables will receive data from the inbound table.

▶ The changelog table is not used in this scenario, hence there is space saving involved when this type of model is used.

▶ Reporting will be based on the active table.

Before the activation process is triggered, make sure that the datatargets get loaded via the inbound table. If that does not happen, the inbound table will be emptied after the activation process.

The reason to utilize this model is to create a corporate memory layer, which would remain the single source of truth for that dataset. This aDSO can also be used for reporting and is also compressed in nature, hence needs less storage space.

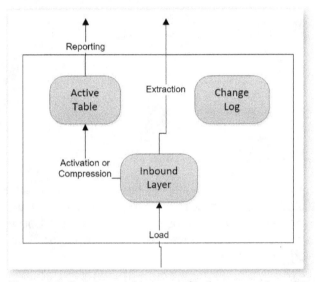

Figure 6.2: Database table usage for the corporate memory—compression capabilities model

Figure 6.2 depicts an inbound table that is utilized to load data into, and to feed data to, other targets. Data is then fed into the active table where data gets compressed or activated.

6.1.1 Functionality

▶ Two tables are used; the inbound table loads data into the data warehouse and feeds the active table and other datatargets.

▶ A changelog table is not filled in, hence there is space saving involved.

▶ Although the system does not use the changelog table, it still creates this table so that system adjustments can be done easily at a later point in time, if the usage of the aDSO changes.

▶ This model is just like the write-optimized DSO, but in this case, reporting is still possible.

▶ Reporting can be done on this object as the data is stored against the semantic key.

6.1.2 Recommended use of this model

▶ As the changelog is not used, the activation process is faster. Load time will not be as fast as the first template, but it is still faster than the other templates.

▶ As data is reportable, this is better than the first model.

6.1.3 How to create an aDSO of the type—corporate memory—compression capabilities

This section shows how an aDSO, based on the corporate memory—compression capabilities model can be created in SAP BW using SAP HANA Studio.

1. Log on to SAP HANA Studio with your SAP BW credentials and go to the InfoArea where you want to create the aDSO.

2. Right-click on the InfoArea and then select NEW • DATASTORE OBJECT (ADVANCED), as shown in Figure 6.3.

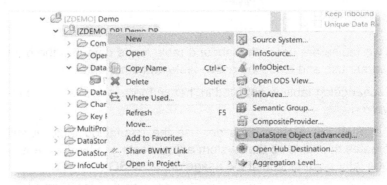

Figure 6.3: Step to create a new aDSO

3. After you choose the option to create an aDSO, the screen shown in Figure 6.4, pops up.

Package:*	$TMP	Browse...
InfoArea:*	ZDEMO_DR	Browse...
☐ Add to Favorites		
Name:*	ZADSO_2	
Description:		
Copy From:		Browse...
Templates		
◉ None		
○ DataSource		
DataSource:		Browse...
Source System:*		Browse...
○ InfoProvider		Browse...
○ InfoSource		Browse...
⑦	Finish	Cancel

Figure 6.4: Create a new Advanced Data Store Object

4. Enter the technical name for the aDSO. In this exercise, the name of the aDSO has been chosen as ZADSO_2. After naming the aDSO, click FINISH.

5. The next screen asks for either the modeling properties (on the left-hand side) or the template model (on the right-hand side). By default, the boxes for ACTIVATE DATA and WRITE CHANGE LOG are checked, as shown in Figure 6.5.

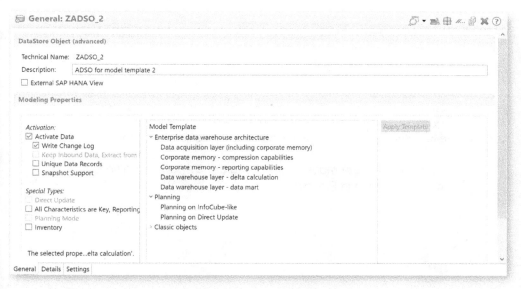

Figure 6.5: Default modeling properties chosen by the system

6. Click on the second template model, CORPORATE MEMORY—COMPRESSION CAPABILITIES • APPLY TEMPLATE.

7. Once the template is applied, the checkboxes for ACTIVATE DATA appear and the checkbox for WRITE CHANGE LOG disappears (as shown in Figure 6.6). This is because the inbound table needs to be loaded and activation is needed for data compression. Also, all data-targets need to be loaded using the inbound table. Although a changelog table gets created in this data model, it is not used by the system. It remains empty.

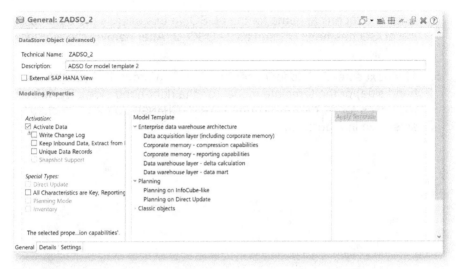

Figure 6.6: Settings for corporate memory—compression capability

8. Once the template model is set, go to the DETAILS tab. The initial screen is shown in Figure 6.7.

Figure 6.7: Initial screen for the details tab

9. Click the ADD FIELD button. Enter the field information as shown in Table 6.1.

Field	Data Type	Length
Order Num	NUMC	10
Order Item	NUMC	4
Product ID	NUMC	18
Order Date	DATE	8
Customer ID	NUMC	10
Order Qty	Decimal	17,2
Order Value	Decimal	17,2

Table 6.1: Fields in an aDSO

Seven fields need to be created. The final screen is shown in Figure 6.8. Note that the MANAGE KEYS button is not greyed out since the active table will have semantic keys instead of technical keys.

Figure 6.8: Details tab for an aDSO

10. Click the MANAGE KEYS button to create a logical key on the aDSO (see Figure 6.9). Choose the following two fields as logic keys: ORDRNUM and ORDERITEM and then click the ADD button. This will add the chosen fields to the KEY section. Click OK.

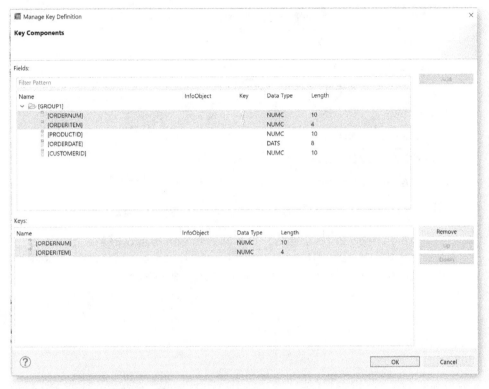

Figure 6.9: Create a logical key for an aDSO

11. Click [Ctrl] + [F3] or the ACTIVATE button ( ).

The aDSO object has now been activated.

12. To analyze how the active, inbound, and changelog tables are being used at the database level, create a flatfile transformation to the aDSO and load a .CSV file into the aDSO. Locate the InfoArea and aDSO ZADSO_2 in RSA1 and create a new transformation with the source as a flatfile datasource and the target as the aDSO. Load the flatfile into the aDSO. (This step is not covered in detail, as this is a regular SQP BW step and is not a new feature.)

13. Once the data gets loaded, log on to the SAP BW administrator workbench and go to TCODE *SE16*. Search for the table *ZADSO_2*. Five tables get listed, as shown n Figure 6.10.

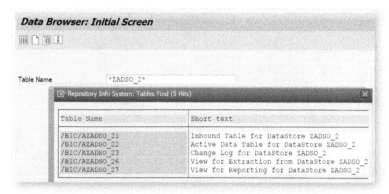

Figure 6.10: Database tables associated with the aDSO

14. Although only the inbound and active tables are being used, the system creates the changelog table. The changelog table remains unused. The other two tables (tables ending with _26 and _27) are views that the system creates for its own usage.

15. The request has been uploaded, but not yet activated. In this situation, a data snapshot for the inbound table, as shown in Figure 6.11, shows the first three fields as: the technical keys request number, datapacket ID, and data record ID.

Data Browser: Table /BIC/AZADSO_21 Select Entries   5

REQTSN	DATAPAKID	RECORD	RECORDMODE	ORDERNUM	ORDERITEM	PRODUCTID	CUSTOMERID	ORDERQTY	ORDERVALUE
20171221221300000001000	000001	1	3	0000000001	0100	0001062016	0000000005	60.00	0.00
20171221221300000001000	000001	2	3	0000000002	0100	0001022016	0000000002	31.98	0.00
20171221221300000001000	000001	3	3	0000000003	0100	0001032016	0000000003	90.00	0.00
20171221221300000001000	000001	4	3	0000000004	0100	0001042016	0000000004	63.96	0.00
20171221221300000001000	000001	5		0000000000	0000	0000000000	0000000000	0.00	0.00

Figure 6.11: Data content for the inbound database table

16. The active and changelog tables are empty, as shown in Figure 6.12 and Figure 6.13.

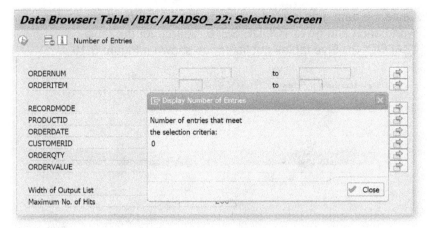

Figure 6.12: Active table is empty

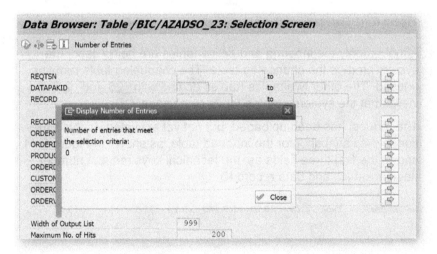

Figure 6.13: Change log table is empty

How to identify active table, changelog table, and inbound table

 For an aDSO, an inbound database table name ends with 1, an active database table name ends with 2, and a changelog database table name ends with 3.

17. Now, right-click on the aDSO and click MANAGE. Click on the loaded request and then click ACTIVATE. Once the activation process is complete, check all three tables to see which rows have data in them.

18. Execute TCODE *SE16* to bring up the active table. Display the active table content, see Figure 6.14.

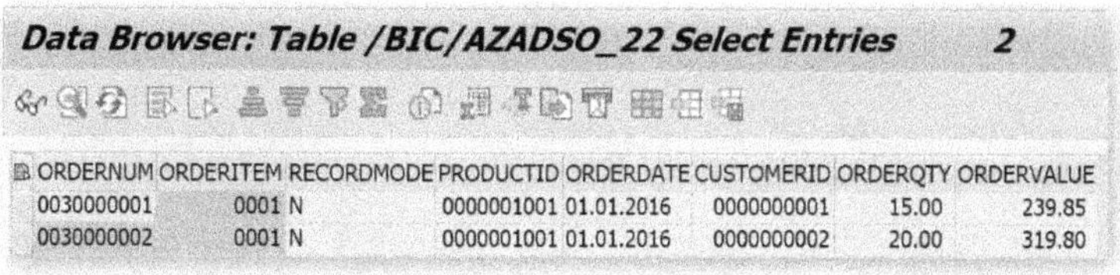

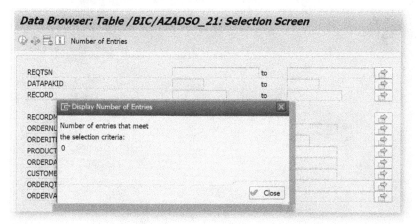

Figure 6.14: Active table content after completing the aDSO data activation

Now check the inbound table content. Right after activation, data from the inbound table should have been pushed into the active table, hence the inbound table should be empty. See Figure 6.15 for the inbound table's record count: it is indeed zero.

Figure 6.15: Inbound table record count after aDSO data activation process

Now check the changelog table. The record count for this table should be zero as this table is not used at all in the activation process, see Figure 6.16.

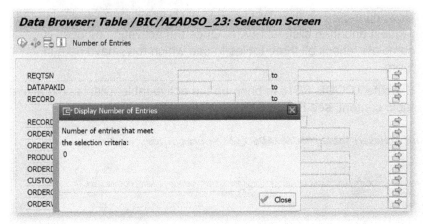

Figure 6.16: Change log record count after aDSO data activation process

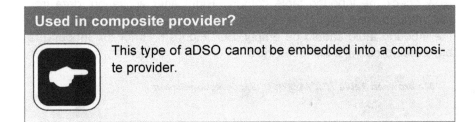

Used in composite provider?

This type of aDSO cannot be embedded into a composite provider.

7 Model template—corporate memory— reporting capabilities

The third template model, corporate memory—reporting capabilities, also deals with the inbound, or loading, layer. Like the first two templates, this model also maintains data at a granular level. It has the modeling properties shown in Figure 7.1.

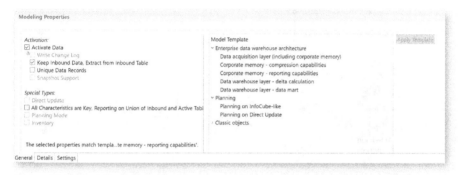

Figure 7.1: Modeling properties for corporate memory—reporting capabilities

When a user chooses this template model, the two modeling properties that are checked are ACTIVATE DATA and KEEP INBOUND DATA, EXTRACT FROM INBOUND TABLE. If the box for ACTIVATE DATA is checked, it means that the data gets loaded into the active table. The box for WRITE CHANGE LOG is unchecked, which means further loading into datatargets does not happen using the changelog. In summary:

▶ The inbound table is used to load data into SAP BW.

▶ When the activation process is kicked off, the data from the inbound table is then loaded into the active table.

▶ As the data in the active table is based on the semantic key, data is compressed (activated) per the key.

▶ The target tables will receive data from the inbound table.

▶ A changelog table is not used in this scenario, hence there is space saving involved when this type of model is used.

▶ Reporting will be based on the active table.

► After loading the active table, data from the inbound table does not get deleted.

The reason to utilize this model is to create a corporate memory layer, which would remain the single source of truth for that dataset. This aDSO can also be used for reporting and is also compressed in nature. This model has data redundancy as data is also retained in the inbound layer. As data is still present in the inbound layer, data can be dropped from the active table and the active table can be restored from the inbound layer.

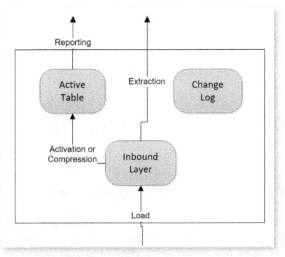

Figure 7.2: Database table usage for the corporate memory—reporting capabilities model

Figure 7.2 depicts that the inbound table is utilized to load data into, and to feed data to, other targets. Data is then fed into the active table where data gets compressed or activated.

7.1.1 Functionality

► This model uses two tables: the inbound table for loading data in the data warehouse and for feeding the active table and other datatargets.

► A changelog table is not filled in, hence there is space saving involved.

▶ Although the system does not use the changelog table, it still creates it so that system adjustments can be done easily at a later point in time, if the usage of the aDSO changes.

▶ Reporting can be done on this object as the data is stored against the semantic key in the active table.

7.1.2 Recommended use of this model

▶ As the changelog is not used, the activation process is faster.

▶ As data is reportable, this is better than the data acquisition layer (including corporate memory) model.

▶ If historical data is needed, this is the model to use, as the inbound table will retain data in the source system.

7.1.3 How to create an aDSO of the type—corporate memory—reporting capability

This section shows how an aDSO, based on the corporate memory—reporting capability model, can be created in SAP BW using SAP HANA Studio.

1. Log on to SAP HANA Studio with your SAP BW credentials and go to the InfoArea where you want to create the aDSO.

2. Right-click on the InfoArea and then select NEW • DATASTORE OBJECT (ADVANCED), as shown in Figure 7.3.

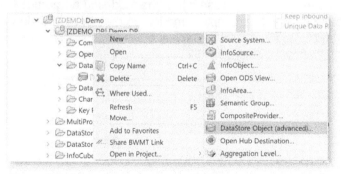

Figure 7.3: Steps to create a new aDSO

3. After you choose the option to create an aDSO, the screen, as shown in Figure 7.4, pops up.

Figure 7.4: Create a new Advanced Data Store Object

4. Enter the technical name for the aDSO. In this exercise, the name of the aDSO has been chosen as ZADSO_3. After naming the aDSO, click FINISH.

5. The next screen asks to choose either the modeling properties (on the left-hand side) or the template model (on the right-hand side). By default, the boxes for ACTIVATE DATA and WRITE CHANGE LOG are checked, as shown in Figure 7.5.

6. Click on the third template model, CORPORATE MEMORY—REPORTING CAPABILITIES • APPLY TEMPLATE.

Figure 7.5: Default modeling properties chosen by the system

7. Once the template is applied, the box for ACTIVATE DATA appears and the box for WRITE CHANGE LOG disappears (as shown in Figure 7.6). This is because the inbound table needs to be loaded and activation is needed for data compression. Also, all datatargets need to be loaded using the inbound table. This is indicated by the checkbox for the option KEEP INBOUND DATA, EXTRACT FROM INBOUND TABLE. Although a changelog table gets created in this data model, it is not used by the system. It remains empty.

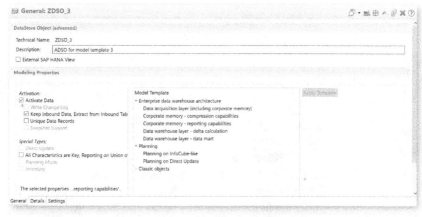

Figure 7.6: Settings for corporate memory—reporting capability

8. Once the template model is set, go to the DETAILS tab. Click the ADD FIELD button. Enter the field information, as shown in Table 7.1.

Field	Data Type	Length
Order Num	NUMC	10
Order Item	NUMC	4
Product ID	NUMC	18
Order Date	DATE	8
Customer ID	NUMC	10
Order Qty	Decimal	17,2
Order Value	Decimal	17,2

Table 7.1: Fields in an aDSO

Seven fields need to be created. The final screen is shown in Figure 7.7. Note that the MANAGE KEYS button is not greyed out as the active table will have semantic keys and not technical keys.

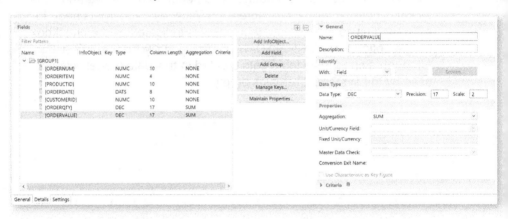

Figure 7.7: Details tab for aDSO

9. Click the MANAGE KEYS button to create a logical key on the aDSO (see Figure 7.8). Choose the following two fields as logic keys: ORDRNUM and ORDERITEM and then click the *ADD* button. This will add the chosen fields to the KEY section. Click *OK*.

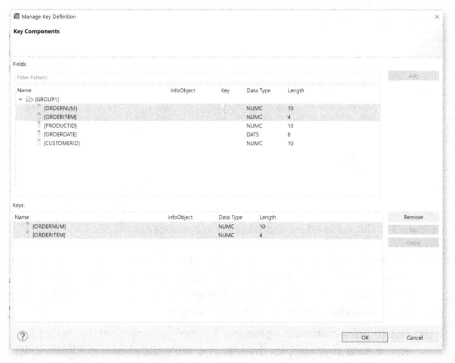

Figure 7.8: Create a logical key for an aDSO

10. Click ⌈Ctrl⌉ + ⌈F3⌉ or the ACTIVATE button (⬚).

11. The aDSO object has now been activated.

12. To analyze how the active, inbound, and changelog tables are being used at the database level, create a flatfile transformation to the aDSO and load a .CSV file into the aDSO. Locate the InfoArea and aDSO ZADSO_3 in RSA1 and create a new transformation with the source as a flatfile datasource and the target as the aDSO. Load a flatfile into the aDSO. (This step is not covered in detail, as this is a regular SAP BW step and is not a new feature.) A sample dataset for this file is given in Appendix 15.1 (File Format).

13. Once the data gets loaded, log on to the SAP BW administrator workbench and go to TCODE *SE16*. Search for the table *ZADSO_3*. Five tables get listed, as shown in Figure 7.9.

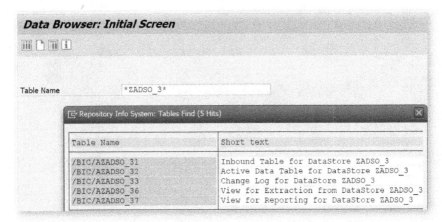

Figure 7.9: Database tables associated with the aDSO

14. Although only the inbound and the active tables are being used, the system creates a changelog table. The changelog table remains unused. Two other tables (tables that end with _36 and _37) are views that the system creates for its own usage.

15. The request has been uploaded, but not yet activated. In this situation, a data snapshot for the inbound table, as shown in Figure 7.10, shows the first three fields as the: technical keys request number, datapacket ID, and data record ID.

Data Browser: Table /BIC/AZADSO_31 Select Entries 2

REQTSN	DATAPAKID	RECORD	RECORDMODE	ORDERNUM	ORDERITEM	PRODUCTID	ORDERDATE	CUSTOMERID	ORDERQTY	ORDERVALUE
20171223010029000001000	000001	1		0030000001	0001	0000001001	01.01.2016	0000000001	15.00	239.85
20171223010029000001000	000001	2		0030000002	0001	0000001001	01.01.2016	0000000002	20.00	319.80

Figure 7.10: Data content for the inbound database table

16. The active and changelog tables are empty, as shown in Figure 7.11 and Figure 7.12.

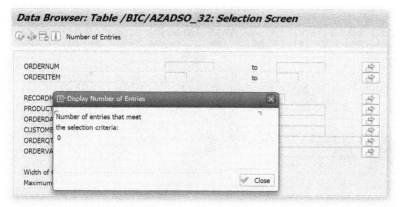

Figure 7.11: Active table is empty

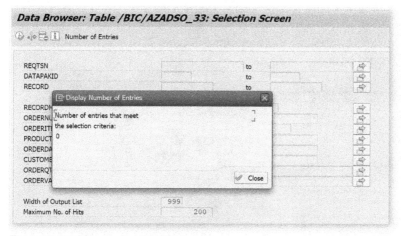

Figure 7.12: Change log table is empty

How to identify active table, changelog table, and inbound table

For an aDSO, an inbound database table name ends with 1, an active database table name ends with 2, and a changelog database table name ends with 3.

81

17. Now, right-click on the aDSO and click MANAGE. Then click on the loaded request, and then ACTIVATE. Once the activation process is complete, check all three tables to see which rows have data in them.
18. Execute TCODE *SE16* to bring up the active table. Display the content of the active table, see Figure 7.13.

ORDERNUM	ORDERITEM	RECORDMODE	PRODUCTID	ORDERDATE	CUSTOMERID	ORDERQTY	ORDERVALUE
0030000001	0001	N	0000001001	01.01.2016	0000000001	15.00	239.85
0030000002	0001	N	0000001001	01.01.2016	0000000002	20.00	319.80

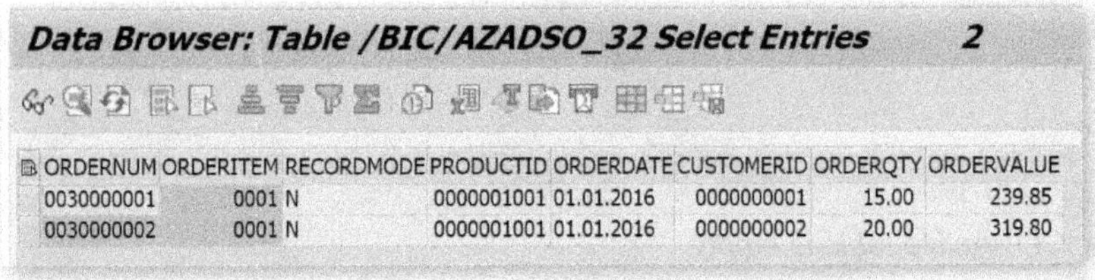

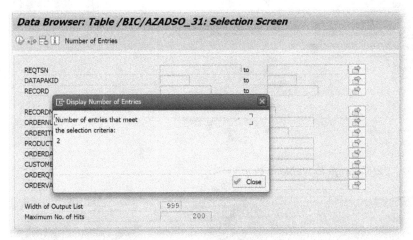

Figure 7.13: Active table content after completing the aDSO data activation

Now check the inbound table content. Figure 7.14 shows the inbound table's record count.

Figure 7.14: Inbound table record count after aDSO data activation process

Now check the changelog table. Record count for this table should be zero as this table is not used in the activation process. See Figure 7.15.

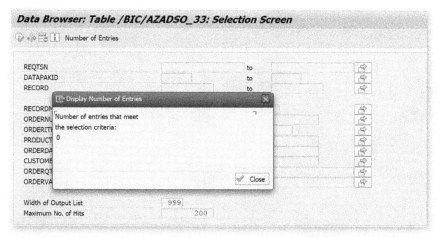

Figure 7.15: Change log record count after aDSO data activation process

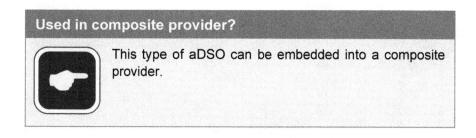

Used in composite provider?

This type of aDSO can be embedded into a composite provider.

8 Model template—data warehouse layer—delta calculation

The fourth template model that SAP has provided for Advanced DSOs, data warehouse layer—delta calculation, provides features similar to the staging layer of a data warehouse. The staging layer extracts data from the inbound, or loading, layer. Before data is stored in this type of aDSO, data should be cleaned and consolidated. It has the modeling properties shown in Figure 8.1.

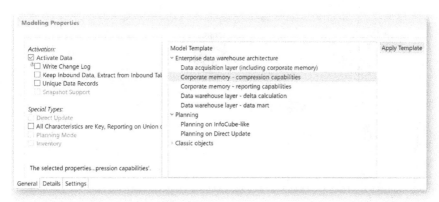

Figure 8.1: Modeling properties for data warehouse layer—delta calculation

When choosing this template model, the two modeling properties that are checked are ACTIVATE DATA and WRITE CHANGE LOG. If the box against ACTIVATE DATA is checked, it means that the data gets loaded into the active table. As the box against WRITE CHANGE LOG is checked, this means that further loading into datatargets takes place using the changelog table instead of the inbound table. In summary:

▶ The inbound table is used to load data into SAP BW.

▶ When the activation process is kicked off, the data from the inbound table is loaded into the active table.

▶ As the data in the active table is based on the semantic key, data is compressed (activated) per the key.

► Reporting will be based on the active table.

► After loading the active table, data from the inbound table gets deleted.

► The activation process compares the data between the inbound table and the active table and then posts a delta image to the changelog table.

► The target tables receive data from the changelog table.

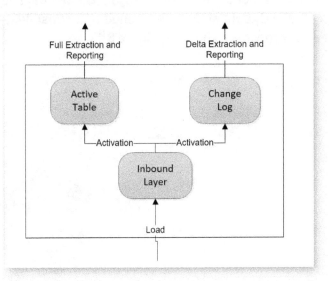

Figure 8.2: Database table usage for the data warehouse layer—delta calculation model

Figure 8.2 depicts that the inbound table is utilized to load data into the active table. Data is then fed into the active table and the changelog table based on the activation process. A changelog table will be used to push delta images to the datatargets. The active table is used for full extraction loads into datatargets

8.1.1 Functionality

► This model uses all three tables. The inbound table is used to load data in the warehouse.

▶ A changelog table is filled in, hence there is no space saving involved.

▶ Reporting can be done on this object as the data is stored against the semantic key in the active table.

▶ This template is similar to the classic DSO.

▶ The UNIQUE DATA RECORDS box can be checked if the source will always send data which does not exist in the active table (semantic key in every load will be unique). If that box is checked, the activation program will not compare data between the inbound and active tables. It will load the delta data from the loading layer as a delta into the active table and to the changelog table.

8.1.2 Recommended use of this model

▶ This template model should be used in the staging layer of a data warehouse.

▶ This type of aDSO can be used for reporting.

▶ This type of aDSO is perfect to feed delta data to the datatargets.

8.1.3 How to create an aDSO of the type—data warehouse layer—delta calculation

This section shows how an aDSO, based on the data warehouse layer—delta calculation model, can be created in SAP BW using SAP HANA Studio.

1. Log on to SAP HANA Studio with your SAP BW credentials and go to the InfoArea where you want to create the aDSO.

2. Right-click on the InfoArea and then select NEW • DATASTORE OBJECT (ADVANCED), as shown in Figure 8.3.

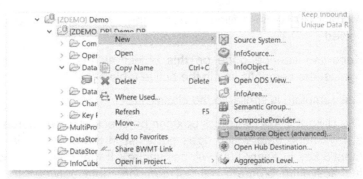

Figure 8.3: Step to create a new Advanced DSO

3. After you choose the option to create an aDSO, the screen, shown in Figure 8.4, pops up.

Figure 8.4: Create a new Advanced Data Store Object

4. Enter the technical name for the aDSO. In this exercise, the name of the aDSO has been chosen as ZADSO_4. After naming the aDSO, click FINISH.

5. The next screen asks to choose either the modeling properties (on the left-hand side) or the template model (on the right-hand side). By

default, the boxes for ACTIVATE DATA and WRITE CHANGE LOG are checked.

6. Click on the fourth template model, DATA WAREHOUSE LAYER—DELTA CALCULATION • APPLY TEMPLATE.

7. Once the template is applied, the boxes for ACTIVATE DATA and WRITE CHANGE LOG remain checked (as shown in Figure 8.5).

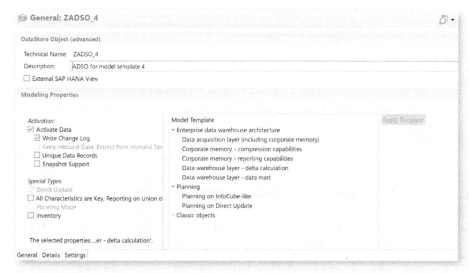

Figure 8.5: Settings for data warehouse layer—delta calculation

8. Once the template model is set, go to the DETAILS tab. Click the ADD FIELD button. Enter the field information, as shown in Table 8.1.

Field	Data Type	Length
Order Num	NUMC	10
Order Item	NUMC	4
Product ID	NUMC	18
Order Date	DATE	8
Customer ID	NUMC	10
Order Qty	Decimal	17,2
Order Value	Decimal	17,2

Table 8.1: Fields in an DSO

Seven fields need to be created. The final screen for fields is shown in Figure 8.6. Note that the MANAGE KEYS button is not greyed out as the active table will have semantic keys instead of technical keys.

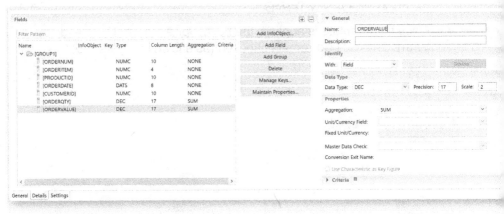

Figure 8.6: Details tab for aDSO

9. Click the MANAGE KEYS button to create a logical key on the aDSO (see Figure 8.7). Choose the following two fields as logic keys: ORDRNUM and ORDERITEM and then click the *ADD* button. This will add the chosen fields to the KEY section. Click *OK*.

Figure 8.7: Create a logical key for an aDSO

10. Click ⌈Ctrl⌉ + ⌈F3⌉ or the Activate button on the top menu bar ( ). The aDSO object has now been activated.

11. To analyze how the active, inbound, and changelog tables are being used at the database level, create a flatfile transformation to the aD-SO and load a .CSV file into the aDSO. Locate the InfoArea and aDSO ZADSO_4 in RSA1 and create a new transformation with the source as a flatfile datasource and the target as the aDSO. Load a flatfile into the aDSO. (This step is not covered in detail, as this is a regular SAP BW step and is not a new feature.) A sample dataset for this file is given in Appendix 15.1.

12. Once the data gets loaded, log on to the SAP BW administrator workbench and go to TCODE *SE16*. Search for the table *ZADSO_4*. Five tables get listed, as shown in Figure 8.8.

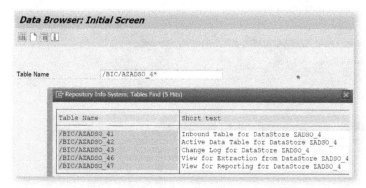

Figure 8.8: Database tables associated with the aDSO

13. The request has been uploaded, but not yet activated. In this situation, a data snapshot for the inbound table, as shown in Figure 8.9, shows the first three fields as the: technical keys request number, datapacket ID, and data record ID.

Data Browser: Table /BIC/AZADSO_41 Select Entries   2

REQTSN	DATAPAKID	RECORD	RECORDMODE	ORDERNUM	ORDERITEM	PRODUCTID	ORDERDATE	CUSTOMERID	ORDERQTY	ORDERVALUE
20171223023557000001000	000001	1		0030000001	0001	0000001001	01.01.2016	0000000001	15.00	239.85
20171223023557000001000	000001	2		0030000002	0001	0000001001	01.01.2016	0000000002	20.00	319.80

Figure 8.9: Data content for the inbound database table

91

14. The active and changelog tables are empty, as shown in Figure 8.10 and Figure 8.11.

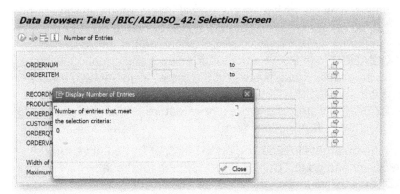

Figure 8.10: Active table is empty

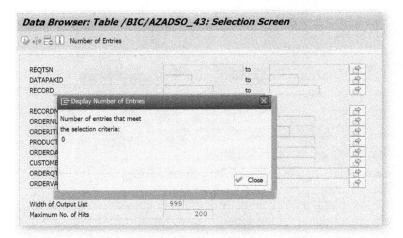

Figure 8.11: Change log table is empty

How to identify active table, changelog table, and inbound table

For an aDSO, an inbound database table name ends with 1, an active database table name ends with 2, and a changelog database table name ends with 3.

15. Now, right-click on the aDSO and click MANAGE. *Then* click on the loaded request, and then ACTIVATE. Once the activation process is complete, check all three tables to see which rows have data in them.
16. Execute TCODE *SE16* to bring up the ACTIVE table. Display the active table content. This is shown in Figure 8.12.

Data Browser: Table /BIC/AZADSO_32 Select Entries 2

ORDERNUM	ORDERITEM	RECORDMODE	PRODUCTID	ORDERDATE	CUSTOMERID	ORDERQTY	ORDERVALUE
0030000001	0001	N	0000001001	01.01.2016	0000000001	15.00	239.85
0030000002	0001	N	0000001001	01.01.2016	0000000002	20.00	319.80

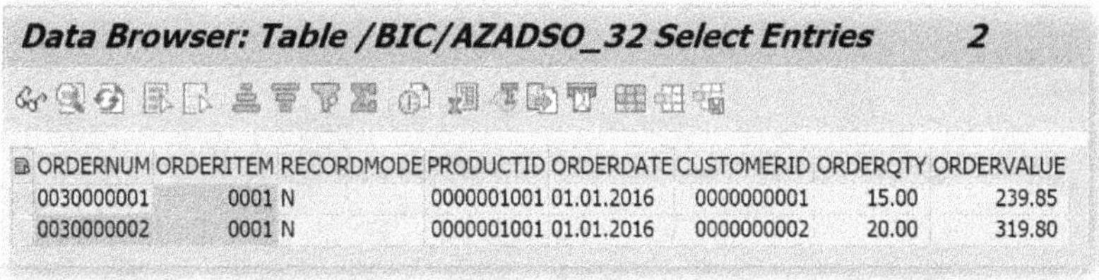

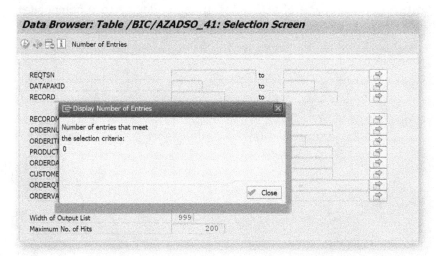

Figure 8.12: Active table content after completing the aDSO data activation

Now check the inbound table content. This model should not have data. See Figure 8.13 for the inbound table's record count.

Figure 8.13: Inbound table record count after aDSO data activation process

Now check the changelog table (see Figure 8.14). The record count for this table should not be zero, as this table is used for storing delta records.

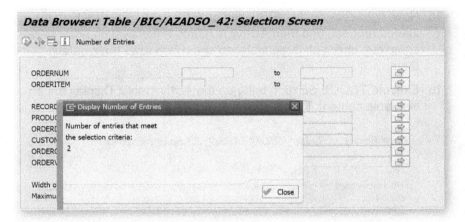

Figure 8.14: Change log record count after aDSO data activation process

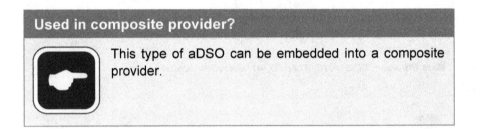

Used in composite provider?

This type of aDSO can be embedded into a composite provider.

9 Model template—data warehouse layer—datamart

The fifth template model that SAP has provided for Advanced DSOs, data warehouse layer—datamart, provides features similar to the reporting layer of a data warehouse. The reporting layer extracts data from the staging layer. Before data is stored in this type of aDSO, data should be cleaned and consolidated. It has the modeling properties shown in Figure 9.1.

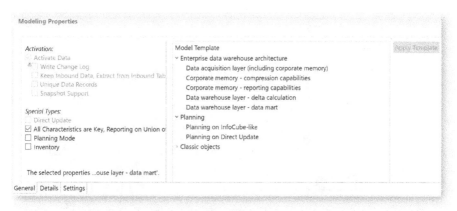

Figure 9.1: Modeling properties for data warehouse layer—datamart

When choosing this template model, the two modeling properties that are checked are ACTIVATE and ALL CHARACTERISTICS ARE KEY, REPORTING ON UNION OF INBOUND AND ACTIVE TABLE. If the box for ACTIVATE is checked, it means that the data gets loaded into the active table. As the box for ALL CHARACTERISTICS ARE KEY, REPORTING ON UNION OF INBOUND AND ACTIVE TABLE is checked, this means that reporting will always combine data from both the inbound table and the active table. In summary:

▶ The inbound table is used to load data into SAP BW.

▶ When the activation process is kicked off, the data from the inbound table is loaded into the active table.

▶ As the data in the active table is based on the semantic key, data is compressed (activated) per the key.

95

▶ Reporting will be based on the active table and inbound table.

▶ After loading the active table, data from the inbound table gets deleted.

▶ The activation process shifts the delta data from the inbound table to the active table.

▶ The changelog table is not filled in—you cannot delete data on a request basis, but you can selectively delete data from the cube.

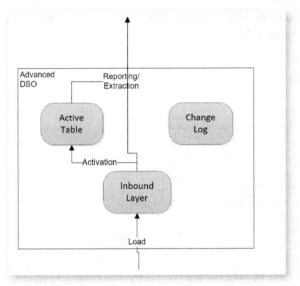

Figure 9.2: Database table usage for the data warehouse layer—datamart model

Figure 9.2 depicts that the inbound table is utilized to load data into the active table, which is combined with the inbound table for reporting purposes. Delta data is fed from this object to other datatargets using the active and inbound tables. A changelog table is not used to feed deltas. This DSO is assumed to be filled in via another DSO similar to a classic DSO, hence deltas generated by this aDSO are assumed to be pre-generated by the source for this aDSO.

9.1.1 Functionality

▶ This model use only two tables and the inbound table is used to load data in the warehouse.

▶ There is space saving involved as a changelog table is not used in this model.

▶ This object is mainly meant for reporting.

▶ This template is similar to the classic InfoCube.

9.1.2 Recommended use of this model

▶ This template model should be used in the reporting layer of a data warehouse.

9.1.3 How to create an aDSO of the type—data warehouse layer—datamart

This section shows how an aDSO, based on the data warehouse layer–datamart model, can be created in SAP BW using SAP HANA Studio.

1. Log on to SAP HANA Studio with your SAP BW credentials and go to the InfoArea where you want to create the aDSO.

2. Right-click on the InfoArea and then select NEW • DATASTORE OB-JECT (ADVANCED), as shown in Figure 9.3.

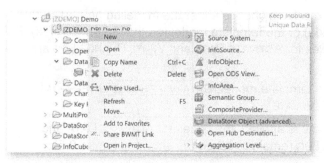

Figure 9.3: Step to create a new aDSO

3. After you choose the option to create an aDSO, the screen, as shown in Figure 9.4, pops up.

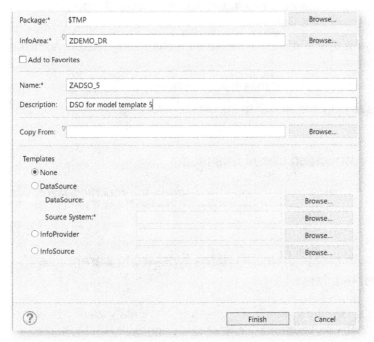

Figure 9.4: Create a new Advanced Data Store Object

4. Enter the technical name for the aDSO. In this exercise, the name of the aDSO has been chosen as ZADSO_5. After naming the aDSO, click FINISH.

5. The next screen asks to choose either the modeling properties (on the left-hand side) or the template model (on the right-hand side). By default, the boxes for ACTIVATE DATA and WRITE CHANGE LOG are checked.

6. Click on the fifth template model, DATA WAREHOUSE LAYER—DATA MART • APPLY TEMPLATE.

7. Once the template is applied, the boxes for ACTIVATE DATA and WRITE CHANGE LOG remain checked (as shown in Figure 9.5).

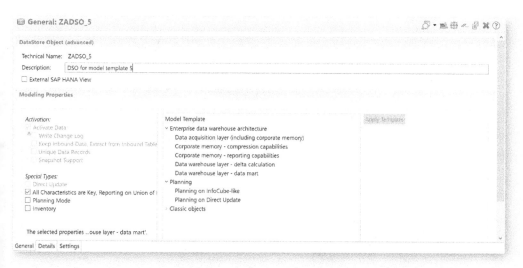

Figure 9.5: Settings for data warehouse layer—datamart

8. Once the template model is set, go to the DETAILS tab. Click the ADD FIELD button. Enter the field information, as shown in Table 9.1.

Field	Data Type	Length
Order Num	NUMC	10
Order Item	NUMC	4
Product ID	NUMC	18
Order Date	DATE	8
Customer ID	NUMC	10
Order Qty	Decimal	17,2
Order Value	Decimal	17,2

Table 9.1: Fields in an aDSO

Seven fields need to be created. The final screen for fields is shown in Figure 9.6. Note that the MANAGE KEYS button is greyed out as this is similar to an InfoCube, where all the characteristics are keys.

Figure 9.6: Details tab for aDSO

9. Click ⌈Ctrl⌉ + ⌈F3⌉ or the ACTIVATE button (▌).

10. The aDSO object has now been activated.

11. To analyze how the active, inbound, and changelog tables are being used at the database level, create a flatfile transformation to the aDSO and load a .CSV file into the aDSO. Locate the InfoArea and aDSO ZADSO_5 in RSA1 and create a new transformation with the source as a flatfile datasource and the target as the aDSO. Load a flatfile into the aDSO. (This step is not covered in detail, as this is regular SAP BW step and is not a new feature.) A sample dataset for this file is provided in Appendix 15.1.

12. Once the data gets loaded, log on to the SAP BW administrator workbench and go to TCODE *SE16*. Search for the table *ZADSO_5*. Five tables get listed, as shown in Figure 9.7.

13. The request has been uploaded, but not yet activated. In this situation, a data snapshot for the inbound table, as shown in Figure 9.8, shows the first three fields as the: technical keys request number, datapacket ID, and data record ID.

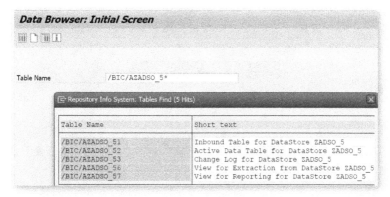

Figure 9.7: Database tables associated with the aDSO

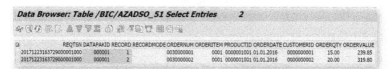

Figure 9.8: Data content for the inbound database table

14. The active and changelog tables are empty, as shown in Figure 9.9 and Figure 9.10.

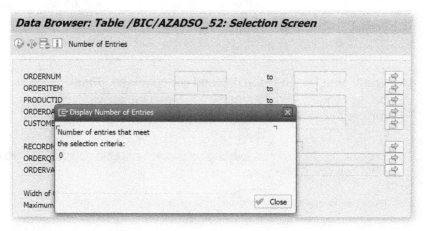

Figure 9.9: Active table is empty

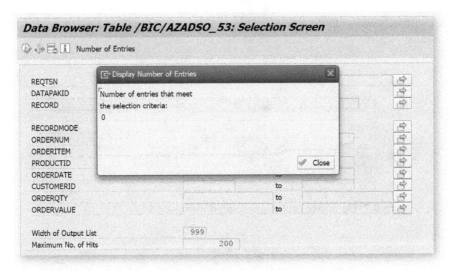

Figure 9.10: Change log table is empty

How to identify active table, changelog table, and inbound table

For an aDSO, an inbound database table name ends with 1, an active database table name ends with 2, and a changelog database table name ends with 3.

15. Now, right-click on the aDSO and click MANAGE. *Then* click on the loaded request and then ACTIVATE. Once the activation process is complete, check all three tables to see which rows have data in them.

16. Execute TCODE *SE16* to bring up the active table. Display the active table content. This is shown in Figure 9.11.

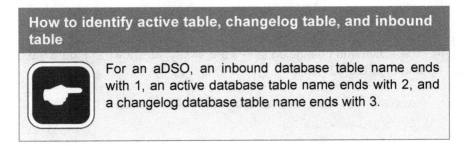

Figure 9.11: Active table content after completing the aDSO data activation

Now check the inbound table content. This model should not have data available, see Figure 9.12.

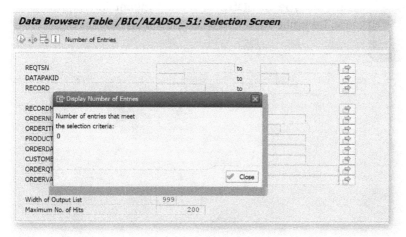

Figure 9.12: Inbound table record count after aDSO data activation process

Now check the changelog table (shown in Figure 9.13). The record count for this table should not be zero, as this table is used for storing delta records.

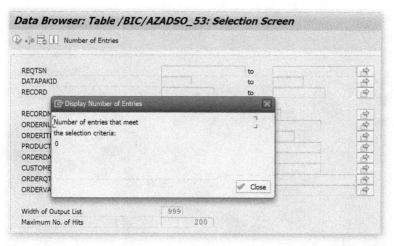

Figure 9.13: Change log record count after aDSO data activation process

Used in composite provider?

 As this type of aDSO is mainly meant for reporting, it can be embedded into a composite provider.

10 Some more features of Advanced DSOs

There are some more features of Advanced DSOs that need to be mentioned, as these features differentiate an aDSO from a classic DSO. With the introduction of the new Advanced DSO, the following features have been introduced by SAP:

- ▶ Field- and InfoObject-based modeling
- ▶ Number of key fields
- ▶ Remodeling with Advanced DSOs
- ▶ Enhanced request management
- ▶ Indexes and partitioning
- ▶ Navigational attributes
- ▶ aDSO lookup in transformation rules
- ▶ External SAP HANA view
- ▶ TCODE RSDWB
- ▶ TCODE RSOADSO

Each of these features is discussed next.

10.1 Field- and InfoObject-based modeling

Before a reporting solution can be created in SAP BW, the basic building blocks have to be created—the InfoObjects. Each and every field has to be first introduced within SAP BW as an InfoObject. Once the InfoObjects are created, they can be used to create DSOs or InfoCubes or any other object in SAP BW. Without InfoObjects, modeling was not possible in SAP BW in non-SAP HANA databases. But, with the introduction of SAP HANA, it's now possible to use fields and InfoObjects to create aDSOs or Open ODS views.

The aDSOs that have been created are all field-based aDSOs. You can add InfoObjects to utilize the power of attributes within reports, for example, when you used the aDSO number five with the model template: DATA WAREHOUSE LAYER–DATAMART. This aDSO was modeled only with fields, as shown in Figure 10.1.

Figure 10.1: An aDSO with field-based modeling

In Figure 10.1, the yellow highlighting shows that it is a field-based model. All the objects listed under GROUP1 are fields. Add another object that is an InfoObject called Sales Organization (0SALESORG) to activate the aDSO. The list of steps is shown in Figure 10.2.

1.   Click the ADD INFOOBJECT button, as shown in Figure 10.2.

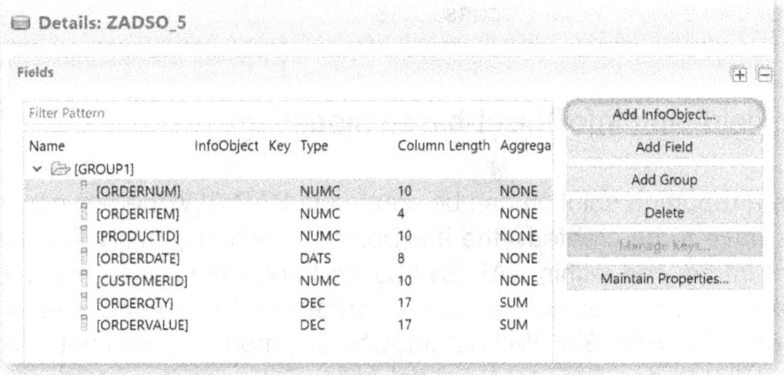

Figure 10.2: Adding InfoObjects to aDSOs

2. Choose the InfoObject called 0SALESORG (shown in Figure 10.3).

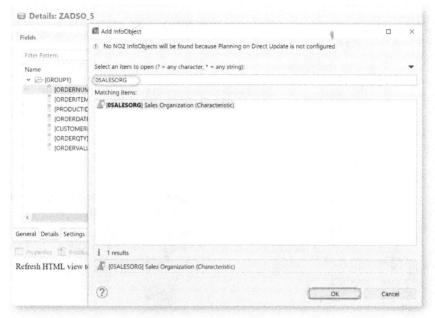

Figure 10.3: Insert an InfoObject into an aDSO

3. After clicking OK, the screen will look like what is shown in Figure 10.4. Activate the aDSO.

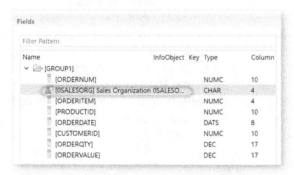

Figure 10.4: An aDSO with fields and InfoObjects

The beauty of utilizing fields in modeling is that to do a quick prototype, you can utilize field-based modeling. The advantage of using InfoObjects in modeling is that it enables the following features of InfoObjects to be utilized while reporting:

▶ InfoObject attributes can be used to provide a more useful report.

▶ Hierarchies created in InfoObjects can be used in reports.

▶ If InfoObjects are authorization relevant, that feature can be automatically used for reporting as well.

10.2 Number of key fields

One of the primary restrictions for a classic DSO was that it could not have more than 16 fields within a key. With the introduction of the SAP HANA database, there is now a maximum of 120 fields or InfoObjects (or a combination of both) within the KEY section of the table. In the old model, InfoCubes were used to bypass this restriction, but this is no longer needed.

10.3 Remodeling with Advanced DSOs

Remodeling is not needed to change an aDSO structurally if it contains no data. If an aDSO contains data, then the SAP BW system provides for a remodeling activity. A modeling screen can be accessed via the TCODE *RSCNV_MONITOR*. While making changes to the aDSO, and if the system needs to create a remodeling request, the changes get collected against the remodeling request. The system gives a warning about the remodeling request. Go to the TCODE for remodeling to activate the changes so that the changes get applied from the M version of the aDSO to the A version. The transport system can only move the A version of aDSO to the target environment.

10.4 Enhanced request management

For the classic DSOs, there is the request management system, as shown in Figure 10.5.

Figure 10.5: Request management for classic DSOs

This management system provides details about the following:

request ID, DTP/InfoPackage, request date, update date, request time, update time, source system, type of data extraction, and whether it has been successfully extracted by the data target or not.

For the Advanced DSOs, the request management system is more elaborate. Figure 10.6 shows the request management screen for an aDSO.

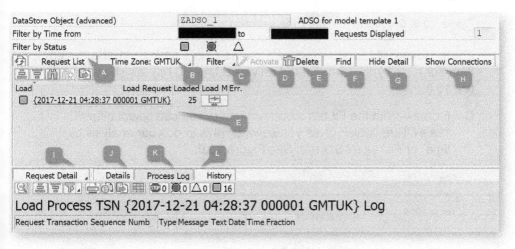

Figure 10.6: Request management for an Advanced DSO

Each of the callouts, labelled with uppercase letters in the image, are explained next.

A. REQUEST LIST—The request list has a dropdown menu that helps further analyze the requests loaded into the system. The request list opens up, as shown in Figure 10.7, to show that requests can be grouped by year, month, or day to do further analysis.

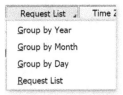

Figure 10.7: Dropdown for request list

B. TIME ZONE—

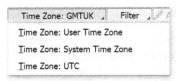

Figure 10.8: Dropdown for time zone selection

There is flexibility to view requests by the user's time zone, the system time zone, or by the coordinated universal time (UTC), as shown in Figure 10.8.

C. FILTER—With the FILTER dropdown menu, you can select either FILTER BY TIME (which gives you several ways to do your analysis by time) or FILTER BY STATUS. See Figure 10.9.

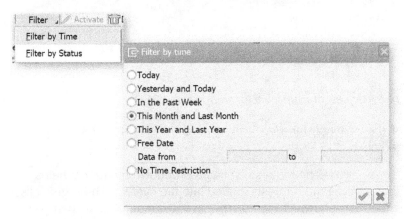

Figure 10.9: Dropdown for filter by time

Figure 10.10 shows analysis by status.

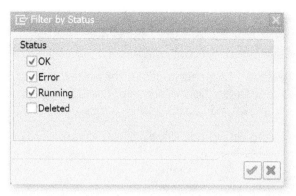

Figure 10.10: Dropdown for filter by status

D. In the classic DSO, the activate option was part of the context menu of the DSO. For aDSO, the request ACTIVATE option is part of the request menu option, as shown in Figure 10.6, callout D.

E. To delete a request, highlight the particular request and then click the DELETE button.

F. FIND—The find option prompts for the request number, as shown in Figure 10.11.

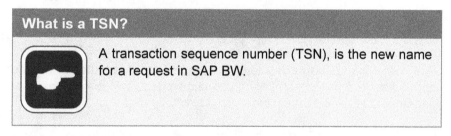

G. Callout G is a toggle that either shows or hides more details for each request loaded. Clicking SHOW DETAIL, opens up a window on the lower half of the screen. Clicking the button once again hides the detail window.

Figure 10.11: Find a request for an aDSO

H. Callout H shows more details about the object's connections: IN-FOPACKAGE, DATASOURCE, and TARGET DETAILS. You can toggle to show or hide more details about the connection.

I. Callout I and J work together. These two options show the load request or the activation request details. A sample of the LOAD RE-QUEST DETAILS option is shown in Figure 10.12.

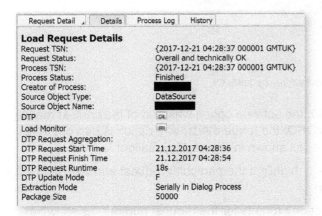

Figure 10.12: Load request details

If you click the DTP button, the DTP opens, and if you click LOAD MONI-TOR, the load monitor opens for that DTP.

The load request shows details of the request that loaded data into the inbound table. The ACTIVATE REQUEST shows details of the request that loaded data into the active table.

J. This option goes along with callout I.

K. The PROCESS LOG is a log generated by the system when a request is being activated.

L. The HISTORY option shows all details about how the system moved data between the inbound, active, and changelog tables.

The request management system, as shown in Figure 10.12, is more detailed than what was provided by SAP for classic DSOs.

10.5 Indexes and partitioning

Indexes—Secondary indexes can be created on an aDSO using the SETTINGS tab for the DSO in SAP HANA Studio. Figure 10.13 shows where this option can be found.

Figure 10.13: Create indexes and partitions for an aDSO

When you click INDEXES, a new screen opens where you can define the type of index that is needed.

Figure 10.14 shows the creation of non-unique index 010 for the InfoObject 0SALESORG for aDSO ZADSO_5.

Figure 10.14: Non-unique index on an aDSO

The index is usually created on the active table. If the active table is not found, the index is created on the inbound table.

CREATION OF INDEX is usually an expert setting and should only be created if there is an issue with query performance on the aDSO.

Partitioning and hash-partitioning are features given by the SAP HANA database to split tables for load balancing. A table cannot contain more than two billion rows. In order to overcome this limitation, a table can be partitioned into different datastores so that each datastore can then hold two billion rows. Figure 10.13 shows where the option to create PARTITIONS can be found in SAP HANA Studio.

10.6 Navigational attributes

Navigational attributes cannot be accessed directly on an aDSO. SAP Note 2185212 gives more details on this topic. In order to create reports that can utilize the navigational attribute feature, a composite provider needs to be created that consumes the aDSO.

10.7 aDSO lookup in transformation rules

Within transformation rules, you can derive characteristic values by looking up InfoObjects and classic DSOs. And now there is the flexibility of doing a similar lookup on an aDSO, as shown in Figure 10.15.

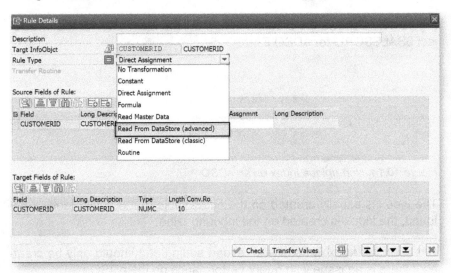

Figure 10.15: Derive characteristic values by looking up aDSOs

10.8 External SAP HANA view

When creating an aDSO, there is also an option to generate the EXTERNAL SAP HANA VIEW. The external SAP HANA view gets generated directly within the SAP HANA database. The view points to the data and tables that are directly managed by SAP BW. This feature has been provided by SAP so that SAP BW tables can be combined with other SAP HANA database tables and views for flexible reporting. Figure 10.16 shows where this feature can be enabled from within SAP HANA Studio.

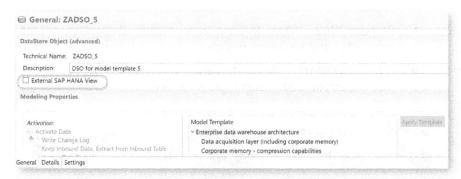

Figure 10.16: Enable external SAP HANA view for an aDSO

10.9 TCODE RSOADSO

Once an aDSO is created via SAP HANA Studio, log into the SAP BW administrator workbench and enter TCODE RSOADSO, and then press ENTER. This will open up a screen, as shown in Figure 10.17.

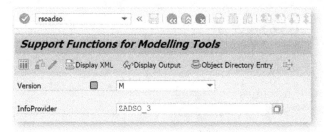

Figure 10.17: TCODE RSOADSO

This screen enables the following:

▶ Display data—Enter the aDSO name in the INFOPROVIDER drop-down, choose version A, and then click the first button for TABLE CONTENTS (▦). This will display data that is contained in that aDSO.

▶ Check—The next button (▨) helps to check if the object is semantically correct.

▶ Activate—The third button from the left (✎) helps to activate the object.

▶ DISPLAY XML—When this object is clicked, it displays the object's XML in a separate window.

▶ DISPLAY OUTPUT—This button shows the data model of the object. A sample in shown in Figure 10.18 for ZADSO_5.

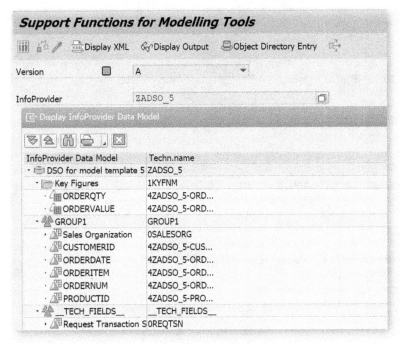

Figure 10.18: Display data model for an aDSO

▶ OBJECT DIRECTORY ENTRY—This option shows the package details of the object (see Figure 10.19). This also helps capture this object in a transport request.

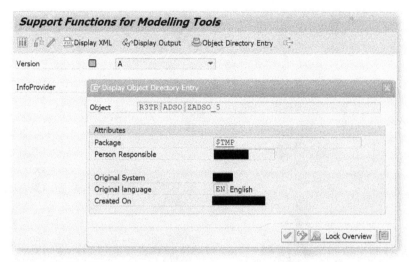

Figure 10.19: Object directory entry screen for an aDSO

▶ Where-used list—The last option on this screen is the WHERE-USED LIST button ( ). Once this button is clicked, it will display all objects that are using this aDSO as a source or as a target. If a composite provider uses this aDSO as a source, the composite provider will get listed. In the case of ADSO_5, the where-used list gets generated, as shown in Figure 10.20. This figure shows that a transformation is connected to the aDSO as a source.

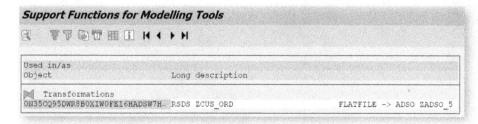

Figure 10.20: Where-used list for an aDSO

11 Comparison of classic DSO with Advanced DSO

After having gone through the various template models and features of aDSOs, it's time to summarize the similarities and differences between classic DSO and Advanced DSO. But first, it's important to discuss classic DSOs. Classic DSO provides SAP BW with a method to store data in a cleansed and consolidated manner. It is a two-dimensional table, which consists of the inbound table, active table, and the changelog table. Data can be stored in the database table to feed a reporting InfoCube or it can be used for reporting.

There are three different types of classic DSOs.

▶ Standard DSO—This is the most commonly used datastore object. It contains and uses all three different tables: the inbound table to collect data from a source; the active table to hold the activated data for reporting; and the changelog table to hold the delta data to be pushed to the datatargets.

▶ Write-optimized DSO—This DSO only contains the inbound table. As quicker turnaround time is needed to load data, write-optimized DSO is chosen as this object does not need activation. Activation is only needed for reporting.

▶ Direct-update DSO—Similar to the write-optimized DSO, this DSO contains only the active table. Data is written into a direct-update DSO via analysis process designer (APD).

Table 11.1 discusses some of the differences and similarities between the classic and Advanced DSOs.

S. No.	Classic DSO on non-SAP HANA platform	Advanced DSO on SAP HANA platform
1	There are three types of classic DSO objects: standard, write-optimized, and direct update	There are five types of core data warehousing DSOs as discussed in previous sections of this book.
2.	Classic DSOs take a long time to activate as they are based on the non-SAP HANA technology.	Advanced DSO activation happens within the SAP HANA database layer. Hence, it is faster than the classic DSO on a non-SAP HANA platform.
3	SAP provides the write-optimized DSO object for faster data-load time.	There are three Advanced DSOs that are used for fast loading: data acquisition layer—including corporate memory, corporate memory—compression capabilities, and corporate memory—reporting capabilities.
4	Once data is activated for a classic DSO, it can be used for reporting.	An Advanced DSO has the type DATA WAREHOUSE LAYER-DATA MART, which is meant for stable reporting.
5	Classic DSOs cannot be embedded within a composite provider.	Advanced DSOs enabled for reporting can be embedded within a composite provider.
6	Indexes can be created on classic DSOs.	Indexes can be created on aDSOs.
7	Modeling of classic DSOs is only via SAP BW administrator workbench.	Modeling of Advanced DSOs can be done only via SAP HANA Studio.
8	Modeling is only possible with InfoObjects.	Modeling is possible with both fields and InfoObjects.
9	Maximum number of objects that can be included as keys is 16.	Maximum number of objects that can be included as keys is 120.
10	Request management for classic DSO is basic.	Enhanced request management is available for aDSOs.
11	Indexes and partitioning are possible with classic DSO.	Indexes and partitioning are possible with aDSO.
12	Reporting is possible with navigational attributes.	Reporting is not possible with navigational attributes.
13	Transformation rules can look up classic DSOs for characteristic derivation.	Transformation rules can look up Advanced DSOs for characteristic derivation.

Table 11.1: Comparison of classic DSO with Advanced DSO

12 Business example 1—analysis of customer spending pattern

A Web-based company sells a lot of products with varying price ranges. The company has a big presence in the United States and its products are popular with the younger generation. There are different categories of goods, some are priced within $20 to $40, some are moderately priced (range of $41 to $100), and some products are priced over $100. As there is a big customer base and the company wants to advertise to customers according to their spending patterns, the company needs to analyze sales data to adhere to the advertising budget appropriately. The company has a Web-based software system that collects real-time data in an Oracle database. The company has SAP BW on SAP HANA for data warehousing and analysis. The database is connected to the SAP BW system using DBCONNECT.

Some points to note:

1. Sales data is collected and stored in the Web-based database.
2. Customer data is collected in the Web-based database.
3. Product data is already stored in the SAP BW system for other reporting requirements.
4. Sales data is more than 100,000 rows of data daily.
5. The customer master data table has more than 50,000 customers and the customer data is growing daily.

Solution for business example 1

1. The order table is shown in Table 12.1. Not all the fields available in the Web-based relational database are needed to analyze the customer spending pattern. The fields shown in the table need to be extracted into SAP BW. This table needs to be stored in SAP BW where the order history can be maintained for analysis.

Field	Datatype	Length
Order Number	CHAR	10
Order Item	CHAR	6
Product ID	CHAR	10
Order Date	DATE	
Customer ID	CHAR	10
Order Type	CHAR	6
Reason	CHAR	6
Order Qty	NUM	17, 2
Order Value	NUM	17, 2

Table 12.1: Details of the order data

2. The order-related fields are as follows:

▶ ORDER NUMBER—This is the order ID against which the order has been captured in the Web-based database. For further enquiries, the user can log on to the Web-based tool to perform further analysis on that particular order number.

▶ ORDER ITEM—Each order might have multiple products against which an order might have been placed. To capture each order item's detail, the order item needs to be extracted into the data warehousing environment.

▶ PRODUCT ID—This is the product number, or the SKU, against which the order has been placed.

▶ ORDER DATE—This is the date the order was placed.

▶ CUSTOMER ID—Each customer is given a unique ID when signing in to the Website for purchasing items for the first time.

▶ ORDER TYPE—This tracks whether a transaction line is a real order or if it is for a customer return. The actual sale is identified by the order type ORD. Return orders are identified by the term RET. Return orders would need to be subtracted to understand the actual sale for each customer.

▶ REASON—Reason for return is tracked in this column. For damaged goods, the identifier is DAMA and for quality-related issues, the identifier is QUAL.

▶ ORDER QUANTITY—This identifies the number of products on the order.

▶ ORDER VALUE—This identifies the total sale value.

3. Customer master data is very important for this company to perform targeted marketing. This object, as shown in Table 12.2, needs to be stored in the corporate memory, so that all changes to the customer master data can be analyzed, if needed.

Field	Datatype	Length
Customer ID	CHAR	10
Gender	CHAR	1
Date of birth	DATS	
Billing Address 1	CHAR	60
Billing Address 2	CHAR	60
Billing City	CHAR	20
Billing State	CHAR	20
Billing Region	CHAR	20
Shipping Address 1	CHAR	60
Shipping Address 2	CHAR	60
Shipping City	CHAR	20
Shipping State	CHAR	20
Shipping Region	CHAR	20
Correspondence Address	CHAR	1
Correspondence Phone	NUM	20
Joining Date	DATS	
Payment Term	CHAR	10

Table 12.2: Details of the customer master data

Note for the address fields: There are two types of addresses captured for the customer. If the shipping address is different from the billing address, then that is captured in a different set of fields.

CORRESPONDENCE ADDRESS is an identifier, either S or B, which identifies whether the shipping address (S) is to be used for correspondence or the billing address (B).

PAYMENT TERM identifies the number of days by which the customer needs to pay the full amount due. 30 means 30 days from order date and 60 means 60 days from order days.

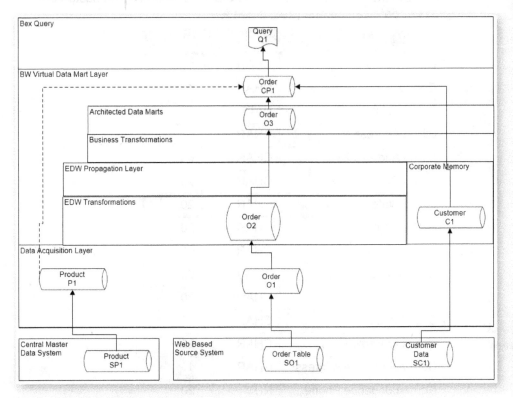

Figure 12.1: LSA++ for the problem in example 1

4. Design the LSA++ for this example problem. To analyze the order and customer data, store the data in an LSA++ which creates a flexible data warehouse environment. A sample LSA++ (based on the company's requirement) is shown in Figure 12.1. To come up with

an LSA++ for your data warehouse, consider the volume of data and frequency of data extracts from the source system.

This is how the LSA++, given in Figure 12.1, can be interpreted. The ORDER TABLE, in the Web-based database, SO1, needs to be extracted into the warehouse. The CUSTOMER DATA table SC1 also needs to be extracted from the same database into the data warehouse. Product table SP1, is centrally maintained in a master data management system, outside of the Web-based database and the data warehouse. That table needs to be extracted into the warehouse as well, for product-related analysis.

5. Product table SP1, can be extracted into the data acquisition layer and stored in an InfoObject called ZDEMO_P1. Enable the attributes to be navigational, so the reports can utilize the attributes for product-related analysis. Keep the InfoObject in the DAL layer, since there is no need to perform any transformation on this object.

6. Customer table SC1, needs to be extracted into the data warehouse. As customer data is very important for the business and is needed for detailed analysis, keep it in the corporate memory. Transfer the data into the data warehouse and store it in an aDSO called ZDEMO_C1.

7. Order data SO1 needs to be extracted from the Web-based system and stored within the data warehouse. Store it in the DAL in an aDSO, as ZDEMO_O1. When transactional data is extracted into the DAL, it is in the source system format. Some of the date and character formats need to be changed and for that, extract ZDEMO_O1 into the EDW transformation layer and store it in aDSO, ZDEMO_O2. From there, extract that directly into another aDSO, called ZDEMO_O3, which sits in the architected datamart layer. Skip the data propagation layer and BTL, as there is no need to perform any BTL or semantic-specific transformations. In the real world, there are many more transformations needed. For this example, it's only necessary to perform transformations in the EDW transformation layer.

8. The order data is then attached to a composite provider called ZDEMO_CP1. This composite provider uses the product and customer data to give a more detailed analysis of the order data.

9. This composite provider is then referred to by the query ZDEMO_Q1, where all data needed for reporting comes together.

This is the query that is then used by the business users to analyze spend data by customer. (Upcoming steps talk more about the details of each object.)

10. Product master data has not been talked about in much detail yet. The product master data in the central master data system has more details, but for this exercise, only consider PRODUCT ID, PRODUCT COST, and PRODUCT TEXT (short, medium, and long). Product details are shown Table 12.3 and Table 12.4.

Field	Datatype	Length
Product ID	CHAR	10
Product Cost	FLTP	17, 2

Table 12.3: Product master (attribute table)

Note: Assumption is that the cost is always in USD.

Field	Datatype	Length
Product ID	CHAR	10
Product Short Description	CHAR	20
Product Medium Description	CHAR	40
Product Long Description	CHAR	60

Table 12.4: Product master (text table)

11. **Product catalog—Create ZDEMO_P1 InfoObject**—Create an InfoObject called ZDEMO_P1 with one attribute InfoObject called ZDEMO_PC1. The data types are given in Table 12.3. Mark the ZDEMO1 InfoObject to have three types of text.

   a. Go to SAP HANA Studio. Create two InfoObjects. Right-click on InfoArea and choose *New • InfoObject*, as shown in Figure 12.2.

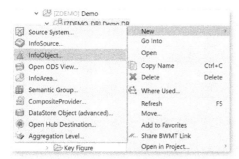

Figure 12.2: Create an InfoObject via SAP HANA Studio

b. Create the InfoObject ZDEMO_PC1 to capture product cost. This should be KEY FIGURE TYPE: NUMBER and DATA TYPE: FLTP. Activate the InfoObject, by clicking the ACTIVATE button ( ). The activated InfoObject is shown in Figure 12.3.

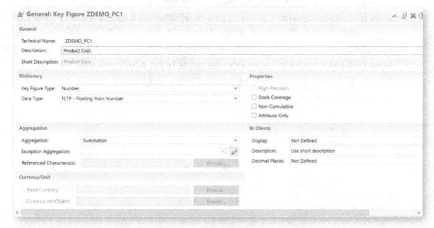

Figure 12.3: Key figure InfoObject ZDEMP_PC1

c. Now create the final InfoObject for the product master data, ZDEMO_P1.

d. Create a new InfoObject, as shown in Figure 12.2 and Figure 12.4. The type of InfoObject to be created is of the type CHARACTERISTIC. Click FINISH.

127

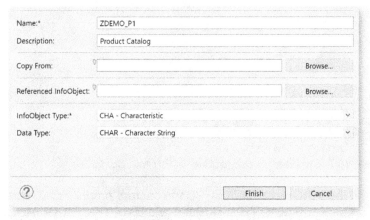

Figure 12.4: Create characteristic InfoObject called product catalog

e.   Within the PROPERTIES section, click the box beside MASTER DATA
     and the box beside TEXTS. This is shown in Figure 12.5. After select-
     ing these items, the additional tab called MASTER DATA/TEXTS gets
     enabled, as shown highlighted in yellow in Figure 12.5. Checking the
     MASTER DATA box allows you to attach an attribute called PRODUCT
     COST. Enabling the checkbox for TEXT enables loading descriptions
     for the product catalog.

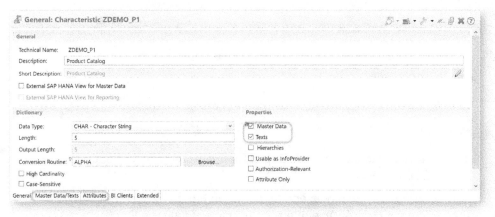

Figure 12.5: Create an InfoObject with attributes and texts

f.   Click the ATTRIBUTES tab and click ADD. Refer to Figure 12.6.

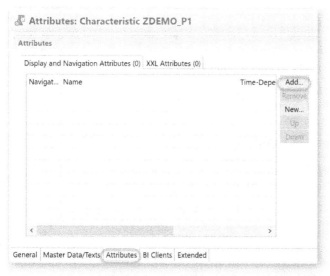

Figure 12.6: Add an attribute to an InfoObject

g. Type in the InfoObject name ZDEMO_PC1 in the window and then once the system shows the object, highlight the object, and then click *OK*. This is shown in Figure 12.7.

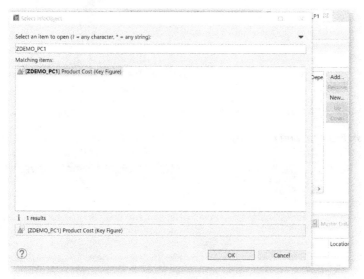

Figure 12.7: Select an attribute for an InfoObject

h. The screen, as shown in Figure 12.9, is displayed with the added InfoObject. Note: This cannot be a navigational attribute, as it is a key figure. If this were a regular characteristic, the system would have allowed the object to be converted into a navigational attribute.

i. Click the MASTER DATA/TEXTS tab and then click the MEDIUM TEXT and LONG TEXT checkboxes (Figure 12.8). This allows the InfoObject to have three different lengths for texts. By default, the short text is the only checkbox switched on.

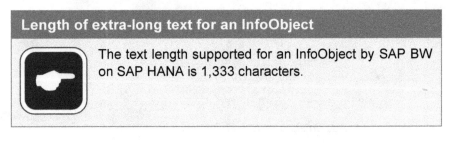

Length of extra-long text for an InfoObject

The text length supported for an InfoObject by SAP BW on SAP HANA is 1,333 characters.

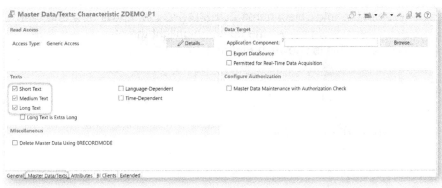

Figure 12.8: Medium and long text enabled for the InfoObject

j. Click the ACTIVATE button. The ZDEMO_P1 object is not active, see Figure 12.9.

130

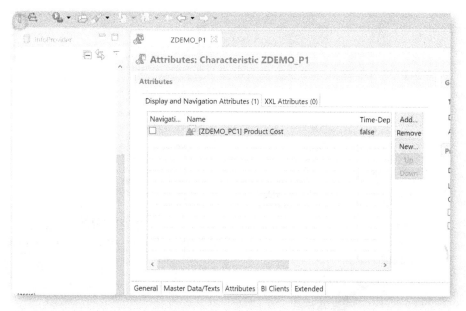

Figure 12.9: Activate the InfoObject ZDEMO_P1

12. **Customer master:** You need to gather the customer master data to analyze all changes that have happened to a customer. Store it in the corporate memory to have the ability to report on the customer master as it was obtained from the source system. Also, you need to design so it can be embedded within a composite provider for further analysis.

    a. Create ZDEMO_C1—This will be an aDSO of the type CORPO-RATE MEMORY–COMPRESSION CAPABILITIES. This model was chosen as there will be a necessity to query this object directly. Embed this as part of the composite provider for customer analysis.

    b. Right-click on the InfoArea, Click NEW • DATASTORE OBJECT (ADVANCED), as shown in Figure 12.10.

131

Figure 12.10: Create an aDSO

c. In the next screen, enter the name of the aDSO, ZDEMO_C1 (see Figure 12.11), with its name as *Customer Master.* After that, click the FINISH button.

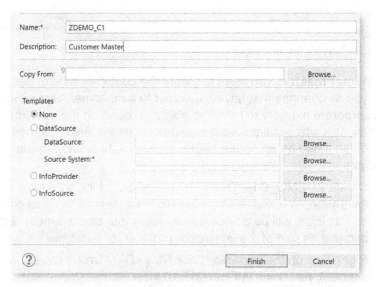

Figure 12.11: Enter details for an aDSO

d. In the next screen (see Figure 12.12), choose the model called COR-PORATE MEMORY—COMPRESSION CAPABILITIES.

Figure 12.12: Choose the template for the aDSO

e. Now add the fields to the aDSO, as listed in Table 12.5 and shown in Figure 12.13.

List of Fields	Datatype	Length	Type of object added
Customer ID	CHAR	10	Field
Gender	CHAR	1	Field
Date of birth	DATS		Field
Billing Address 1	CHAR	60	Field
Billing Address 2	CHAR	60	Field
Billing City	CHAR	20	Field
Billing State	CHAR	20	Field
Billing Region	CHAR	20	Field
Shipping Address 1	CHAR	60	Field
Shipping Address 2	CHAR	60	Field
Shipping City	CHAR	20	Field
Shipping State	CHAR	20	Field
Shipping Region	CHAR	20	Field
Correspondence Address	CHAR	1	Field
Correspondence Phone	NUM	20	Field
Joining Date	DATS		Field
Payment Term	CHAR	10	Field

Table 12.5: List of fields in a customer aDSO

133

Figure 12.13: Add InfoObjects to the aDSO

f.   Click the MANAGE KEYS button and add CUSTOMER ID as the key
(shown in Figure 12.14).

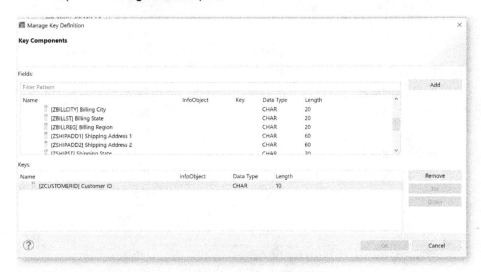

Figure 12.14: Add customer ID as a key for the aDSO

g. Now, click the ACTIVATE ( ) button on the menu bar of SAP HANA Studio.

This completes the creation of the customer master aDSO.

13. **Order data** (DAL)—The following describes how to create the order transaction data objects.

a. The first transactional aDSO to create is for the DAL. In SAP BW, on a non-SAP HANA database, you have used either a standard DSO or write-optimized DSO to create this layer, but with an SAP HANA database, there is more flexibility with different types of aDSOs. Choose the model template DATA ACQUISITION LAYER—INCLUDING CORPORATE MEMORY. This is to hold all the data from the source system. It is not for direct reporting, but is used to feed data to the data warehouse transformation layer. Follow the steps shown in Figure 12.15 to create this aDSO. Name it aDSO ZDEMO_O1.

b. Right-click on the INFOAREA and choose NEW • DATASTORE OBJECT (ADVANCED), as shown in Figure 12.15.

Figure 12.15: Create a new aDSO

c. On the screen that pops up, enter the name of the aDSO, ZDEMO_O1, (shown in Figure 12.16), and click FINISH.

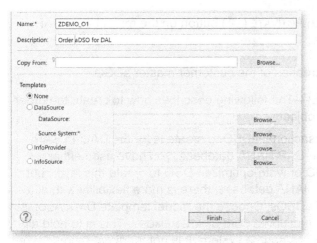

Figure 12.16: Create an aDSO for the DAL

d. Now, choose the template, DATA ACQUISITION LAYER—INCLUDING CORPORATE MEMORY, click APPLY TEMPLATE. This is shown in Figure 12.17.

Figure 12.17: Apply template for the DAL aDSO

e. Click the DETAILS tab.

Fields and InfoObjects

In these examples, I have chosen fields to model the aDSOs and InfoObjects. For your data warehouse, you might want to use InfoObjects.

f. The list of fields that need to be added to the aDSO is shown in Table 12.6.

Field	Datatype	Length	Type of object added
Order Number	CHAR	10	Field
Order Item	CHAR	6	Field
Product ID	CHAR	10	Field
Order Date	DATE		Field
Customer ID	CHAR	10	Field
Order Type	CHAR	6	Field
Reason	CHAR	6	Field
Order Qty	NUM	17, 2	InfoObject (0Quantity)
Unit	Unit	3	InfoObject (0Unit)
Order Value	NUM	17, 2	InfoObject (0AMOUNT)
Currency	CUKY	5	InfoObject (0CURRENCY)

Table 12.6: List of fields for the DAL aDSO

g. Now click the ACTIVATE button ( ) to activate the aDSO.

14. **Order data (EDW–Transformation)**—The second transactional aDSO to create is for the core EDW–transformation layer. In SAP BW, on a non-SAP HANA database, you used a standard DSO to create this layer, but with an SAP HANA database, there is more flexibility with different types of aDSOs. Choose the model template DATA WAREHOUSE LAYER—DELTA CALCULATION. It is not used for direct reporting, but is used to feed data to the layer. Follow the steps

137

shown in Figure 12.18 to create this aDSO. Name it aDSO ZDEMO_O2.

a.   Right-click on the InfoArea and choose NEW • DATASTORE OB-
     JECT (ADVANCED), as shown in Figure 12.18.

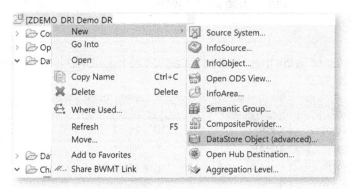

Figure 12.18: Create a new aDSO

b.   On the screen that pops up, enter the name of the aDSO, ZDE-
     MO_O2, indicate that you want to COPY FROM the aDSO ZDE-
     MO_O1, and click FINISH. This is shown in Figure 12.19.

Figure 12.19: Create an aDSO for the DAL

138

c. Now, rename the aDSO to *Order DSO for Transformation Layer.*

d. Choose the template, DATA WAREHOUSE LAYER—DELTA CALCULA-
TION, click APPLY TEMPLATE. This is shown in Figure 12.20.

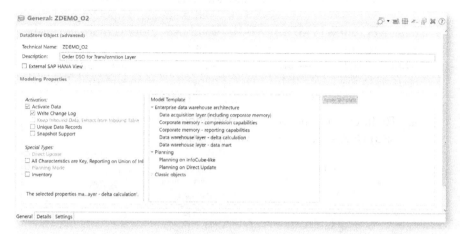

Figure 12.20: Apply the template for the EDW—transformation layer aDSO

e. All the fields are already added into this aDSO, as it was copied
from ZDEMO_O1.

f. Click the DETAILS tab, click the MANAGE KEYS button, and add the
two fields ORDER NUMBER and ORDER ITEM as keys. The DAL
aDSO had the technical keys as the key, but in this type of aD-
SO, you need to add semantic keys. The two key fields are
shown in the DETAILS screen, see Figure 12.21.

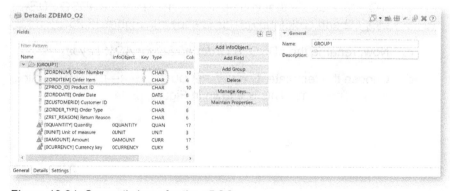

Figure 12.21: Semantic keys for the aDSO

g. Now click the ACTIVATE button (🔲) to activate the aDSO.

15. **Order data (architected datamart layer)**—The third transactional aDSO to create is for the architected datamart layer. In SAP BW, on a non-SAP HANA database, you used a standard InfoCube to create this layer, but with an SAP HANA database, there is more flexibility with different types of aDSOs. Choose the model template DATA WAREHOUSE LAYER—DATAMART. It is not used for direct reporting, but is used to feed data to the layer. Follow the steps shown in Figure 12.22 to create this aDSO. Name it ZDEMO_O3.

a. Right-click on the InfoArea and choose NEW • DATASTORE OBJECT (ADVANCED), as shown in Figure 12.22.

Figure 12.22: Create a new aDSO

b. On the screen that pops up, enter the name of the aDSO, ZDEMO_O3, indicate that you want to COPY FROM the aDSO ZDEMO_O2 and click FINISH. This is shown in Figure 12.23.

c. Now, rename the aDSO to *Order aDSO for ADM Layer.*

d. Choose the template, DATA WAREHOUSE LAYER—DATAMART, click APPLY TEMPLATE. This is shown in Figure 12.24

140

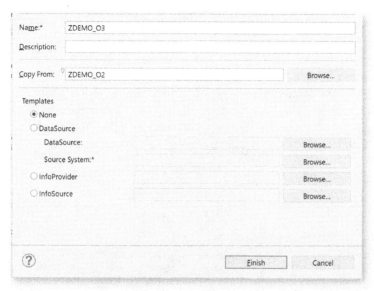

Figure 12.23: Create an aDSO for the ADM Layer

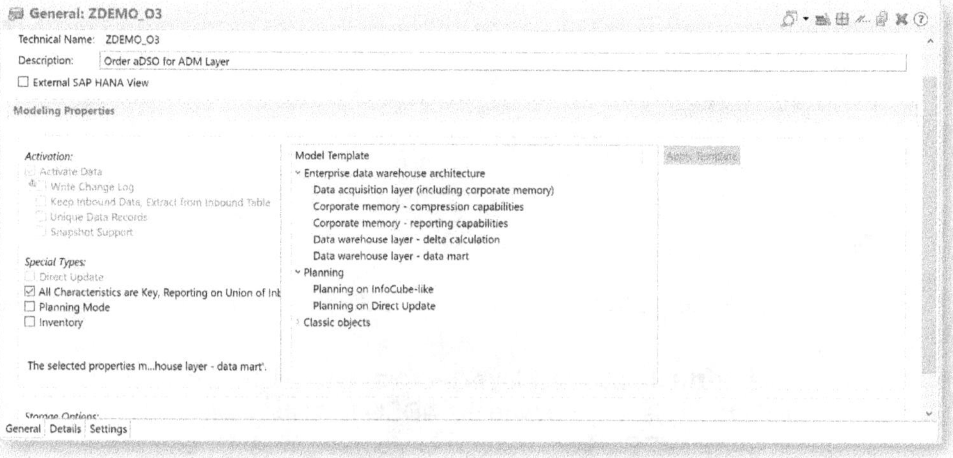

Figure 12.24: Apply template for the ADM layer aDSO

e. All the fields are already added into this aDSO, as it was copied from ZDEMO_O2.

f. Organize the InfoObjects into proper groups to prepare for the reporting layer. Look at Figure 12.25 for the group details. Instead of having one group called GROUP1, there are five groups: order details, customer, product, key figures, and units. After creating the groups (by clicking ADD GROUP in the DETAILS tab), drag and drop the fields or InfoObjects to the proper group.

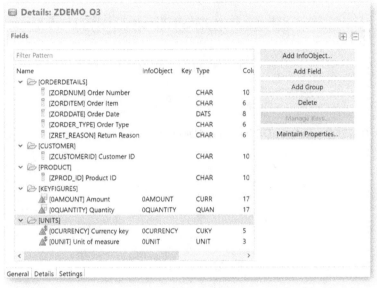

Figure 12.25: Create groups in the aDSO

g. Now click the ACTIVATE button ( ) to activate the aDSO.

16. **Order data (virtual datamart layer)**—This layer will hold the composite provider. This will combine the aDSO from the ADM layer and customer master aDSO from the corporate memory layer, and present a consolidated view to the BEx query layer.

a. Right-click on the InfoArea and choose NEW • COMPOSITEPROVIDER, as shown in Figure 12.26.

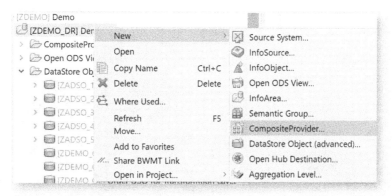

Figure 12.26: Create a new composite provider

b. The next screen (shown in Figure 12.27) that pops up is for entering the technical name of the composite provider and its description.

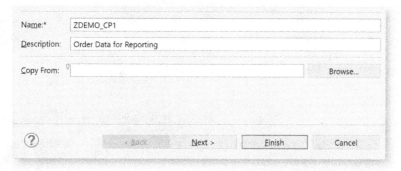

Figure 12.27: Name the composite provider ZDEMO_CP1

c. The next screen asks for the details of the part providers for the composite provider. Join the order data with the customer data in such a manner that it always displays order data, irrespective of the customer data. Use JOIN PROVIDERS instead of UNION PROVIDERS, as shown in the screen in Figure 12.28.

Figure 12.28: Insert part provider as join provider

d. After clicking ADD, click OK. This is shown in Figure 12.29.

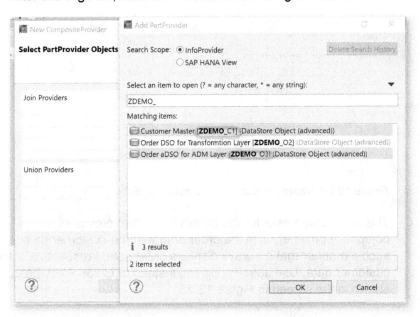

Figure 12.29: Insert ZDEMO_O3 and ZDEMO_C1 as the part provider

e. On the next screen, choose the SCENARIO TAB; a screen is displayed as shown in Figure 12.30.

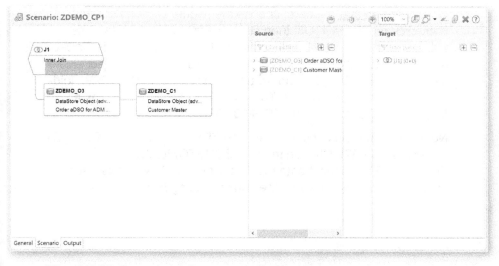

Figure 12.30: Scenario tab for a composite provider

f.   The default join type is an inner join. Change the join type by right-clicking J1 • JOIN TYPE • *Left Outer,* as shown in Figure 12.31. Choose left outer join because everything needs to be displayed from the orders table, irrespective of whether customer master data table has customer records or not.

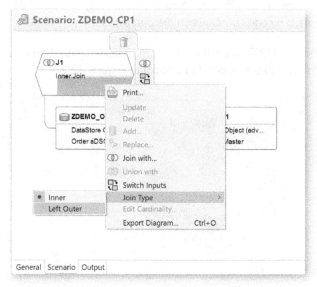

Figure 12.31: Choose left outer join instead of inner join

g. On the screen that appears, choose the middle section (SOURCE), right-click on ZDEMO_O3, then click CREATE ASSIGNMENTS. This step automatically pushes all fields and InfoObjects from the SOURCE section to the TARGET section for the InfoProvider. Now select all fields under ZDEMO_C1 and drop the fields into the CUSTOMER folder of the composite provider. The composite provider now has all fields from ZDEMO_C1 and ZDEMO_O3.

h. Now create the join condition between ZDEMO_O3 and ZDEMO_C1 (see Figure 12.32). Choose the field ZCUSTOMERID from ZDEMO_O3 and drop it onto the TARGET • JOIN CONDITIONS FIELD. A screen pops up that asks for the corresponding field from ZDEMO_C1.

Figure 12.32: Choose join condition between the part providers

i. Choose the ZCUSTOMERID field from ZDEMO_C1. The final join condition looks like what is shown in Figure 12.33.

Figure 12.33: Join conditions of the part providers

146

j. Now click the ACTIVATE button ( ) to activate the composite provider.

17. Load data into ZDEMO_C1, ZDEMO_P1, and ZDEMO_O1. For this example, load the data using a flatfile. In a real scenario, you will connect the tables from your source system using datasources.

  a. Load ZDEMO_C1—As steps to create flatfile datasources is the same for SAP BW on SAP HANA as in SAP BW on non-SAP HANA, those steps are not discussed here. Load the sample data as shown in Appendix 15.2. In order to convert the BILLING STATE CODE and BILLING REGION from lowercase to uppercase, use the following formula: TOUPPER(STRING). Figure 12.34 shows the data that has been loaded via a flatfile into the aDSO.

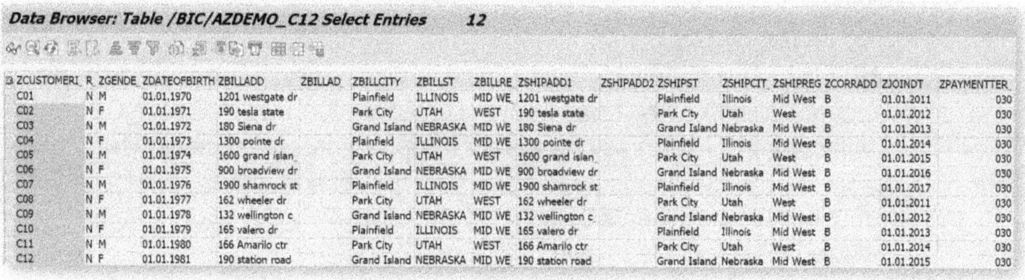

Data Browser: Table /BIC/AZDEMO_C12 Select Entries   12

ZCUSTOMERI	R	ZGENDE	ZDATEOFBIRTH	ZBILLADD	ZBILLAD	ZBILLCITY	ZBILLST	ZBILLRE	ZSHIPADD1	ZSHIPADD2	ZSHIPST	ZSHIPCIT	ZSHIPREG	ZCORRADD	ZJOINDT	ZPAYMENTTER
C01	N	M	01.01.1970	1201 westgate dr		Plainfield	ILLINOIS	MID WE	1201 westgate dr		Plainfield	Illinois	Mid West	B	01.01.2011	030
C02	N	F	01.01.1971	190 tesla state		Park City	UTAH	WEST	190 tesla state		Park City	Utah	West	B	01.01.2012	030
C03	N	M	01.01.1972	180 Siena dr		Grand Island	NEBRASKA	MID WE	180 Siena dr		Grand Island	Nebraska	Mid West	B	01.01.2013	030
C04	N	F	01.01.1973	1300 pointe dr		Plainfield	ILLINOIS	MID WE	1300 pointe dr		Plainfield	Illinois	Mid West	B	01.01.2014	030
C05	N	M	01.01.1974	1600 grand islan		Park City	UTAH	WEST	1600 grand islan		Park City	Utah	West	B	01.01.2015	030
C06	N	F	01.01.1975	900 broadview dr		Grand Island	NEBRASKA	MID WE	900 broadview dr		Grand Island	Nebraska	Mid West	B	01.01.2016	030
C07	N	M	01.01.1976	1900 shamrock st		Plainfield	ILLINOIS	MID WE	1900 shamrock st		Plainfield	Illinois	Mid West	B	01.01.2017	030
C08	N	F	01.01.1977	162 wheeler dr		Park City	UTAH	WEST	162 wheeler dr		Park City	Utah	West	B	01.01.2011	030
C09	N	M	01.01.1978	132 wellington c		Grand Island	NEBRASKA	MID WE	132 wellington c		Grand Island	Nebraska	Mid West	B	01.01.2012	030
C10	N	F	01.01.1979	165 valero dr		Plainfield	ILLINOIS	MID WE	165 valero dr		Plainfield	Illinois	Mid West	B	01.01.2013	030
C11	N	M	01.01.1980	166 Amarilo ctr		Park City	UTAH	WEST	166 Amarilo ctr		Park City	Utah	West	B	01.01.2014	030
C12	N	F	01.01.1981	190 station road		Grand Island	NEBRASKA	MID WE	190 station road		Grand Island	Nebraska	Mid West	B	01.01.2015	030

Figure 12.34: Loaded data in ZDEMO_C1

  b. Load ZDEMO_P1—As the steps to create flatfile datasources is the same for SAP BW on SAP HANA as in SAP BW on non-SAP HANA, they are not discussed here. Load the sample data as shown in Appendix 15.3.

  c. Load ZDEMO_O1—As the steps to create flatfile datasources is the same for SAP BW on SAP HANA as in SAP BW on non-SAP HANA, they are not discussed here. Load the sample data as shown in Appendix 15.4. The loaded data is shown in Figure 12.35.

Data Browser: Table /BIC/AZDEMO_O11 Select Entries   27

REQTSN	DATAPAKID	RECORD	RECORDMODE	ZORDNUM	ZORDITEM	ZPROD_ID	ZORDDATE	ZCUSTOMERID	ZORDER_TYPE	ZRET_REASON	QUANTITY	UNIT	AMOUNT	CURRENCY
20171230011147000001000	000001	1		30000001	1	P1001	01.01.2016	C01	Ord	Ord	15	EA	900.00	USD
20171230011147000001000	000001	2		30000002	1	P1001	01.02.2016	C02	Ord	Ord	20	EA	1,200.00	USD
20171230011147000001000	000001	3		30000003	1	P1001	01.03.2016	C03	Ord	Ord	100	EA	6,000.00	USD
20171230011147000001000	000001	4		30000003	2	P1002	01.04.2016	C04	Ord	Ord	2	EA	60.00	USD
20171230011147000001000	000001	5		30000003	3	P1003	01.05.2016	C05	Ord	Ord	10	EA	1,200.00	USD
20171230011147000001000	000001	6		30000003	4	P1004	01.06.2016	C06	Ord	Ord	20	EA	140.00	USD
20171230011147000001000	000001	7		30000007	1	P1005	01.07.2016	C07	Ord	Ord	30	EA	2,400.00	USD
20171230011147000001000	000001	8		30000008	1	P1004	01.01.2016	C08	Ord	Ord	1	EA	7.00	USD
20171230011147000001000	000001	9		30000008	2	P1001	01.02.2016	C09	Ord	Ord	2	EA	120.00	USD
20171230011147000001000	000001	10		30000008	3	P1002	01.03.2016	C10	Ord	Ord	3	EA	90.00	USD
20171230011147000001000	000001	11		30000008	4	P1001	01.04.2016	C11	Ord	Ord	4	EA	240.00	USD
20171230011147000001000	000001	12		30000012	1	P1002	01.05.2016	C12	Ord	Ord	5	EA	150.00	USD
20171230011147000001000	000001	13		30000013	1	P1003	01.06.2016	C01	Ord	Ord	15	EA	1,800.00	USD
20171230011147000001000	000001	14		30000014	1	P1004	01.07.2016	C02	Ord	Ord	20	EA	140.00	USD
20171230011147000001000	000001	15		30000015	1	P1004	01.01.2016	C03	Ord	Ord	100	EA	700.00	USD
20171230011147000001000	000001	16		30000016	1	P1001	01.02.2016	C04	Ord	Ord	2	EA	120.00	USD
20171230011147000001000	000001	17		30000017	1	P1002	01.03.2016	C05	Ord	Ord	10	EA	300.00	USD
20171230011147000001000	000001	18		30000018	1	P1003	01.04.2016	C06	Ord	Ord	20	EA	2,400.00	USD
20171230011147000001000	000001	19		30000019	1	P1002	01.01.2016	C07	Ord	Ord	30	EA	900.00	USD
20171230011147000001000	000001	20		30000020	1	P1003	01.02.2016	C08	Ord	Ord	1	EA	120.00	USD
20171230011147000001000	000001	21		30000021	1	P1004	01.03.2016	C09	Ord	Ord	2	EA	14.00	USD
20171230011147000001000	000001	22		30000022	1	P1002	01.04.2016	C10	Ord	Ord	3	EA	90.00	USD
20171230011147000001000	000001	23		30000023	1	P1003	01.05.2016	C11	Ord	Ord	4	EA	480.00	USD
20171230011147000001000	000001	24		30000024	1	P1004	01.06.2016	C12	Ord	Ord	5	EA	35.00	USD
20171230011147000001000	000001	25		50000001	1	P1001	01.01.2016	C01	Ret	Dama	5	EA	300.00	USD
20171230011147000001000	000001	26		50000002	1	P1001	01.02.2016	C02	Ret	Qual	2	EA	120.00	USD
20171230011147000001000	000001	27		50000003	1	P1001	01.03.2016	C03	Ret	Dama	10	EA	600.00	USD

Figure 12.35: Data loaded into ZDEMO_O1 aDSO

d. Load ZDEMO_O2—Loading from ZDEMO_O1 into ZDEMO_O2 will convert lowercase characters to uppercase characters. The TOUPPER formula is used to do this conversion in the transformation rule between ZDEMO_O1 and ZDEMO_O2. Data loaded into ZDEMO_O2 is shown in Figure 12.36.

e. Load ZDEMO_O3—This load does not do any conversion. It is a direct load from ZDEMO_O2. Data loaded into ZDEMO_O2 is shown in Figure 12.36.

Data loads

 All the data loads into objects ZDEMO_P1, ZDEMO_C1, ZDEMO_O1, ZDEMO_O2, and ZDEMO_O3 have been done using the SAP BW administrator workbench tool instead of SAP HANA Studio.

Data Browser: Table /BIC/AZDEMO_O32 Select Entries   27

ZORDNUM	ZORDITEM	ZORDDATE	ZORDER_TYPE	ZRET_REASON	ZCUSTOMERID	ZPROD_ID	CURRENCY	UNIT	RECORDMODE	AMOUNT	QUANTITY
30000001	1	01.01.2016	ORD	ORD	C01	P1001	USD	EA	N	900.00	15
30000002	1	01.02.2016	ORD	ORD	C02	P1001	USD	EA	N	1,200.0	20
30000003	1	01.03.2016	ORD	ORD	C03	P1001	USD	EA	N	6,000.0	100
30000003	2	01.04.2016	ORD	ORD	C04	P1002	USD	EA	N	60.00	2
30000003	3	01.05.2016	ORD	ORD	C05	P1003	USD	EA	N	1,200.0	10
30000003	4	01.06.2016	ORD	ORD	C06	P1004	USD	EA	N	140.00	20
30000007	1	01.07.2016	ORD	ORD	C07	P1005	USD	EA	N	2,400.0	30
30000008	1	01.01.2016	ORD	ORD	C08	P1004	USD	EA	N	7.00	1
30000008	2	01.02.2016	ORD	ORD	C09	P1001	USD	EA	N	120.00	2
30000008	3	01.03.2016	ORD	ORD	C10	P1002	USD	EA	N	90.00	3
30000008	4	01.04.2016	ORD	ORD	C11	P1001	USD	EA	N	240.00	4
30000012	1	01.05.2016	ORD	ORD	C12	P1002	USD	EA	N	150.00	5
30000013	1	01.06.2016	ORD	ORD	C01	P1003	USD	EA	N	1,800.0	15
30000014	1	01.07.2016	ORD	ORD	C02	P1004	USD	EA	N	140.00	20
30000015	1	01.01.2016	ORD	ORD	C03	P1004	USD	EA	N	700.00	100
30000016	1	01.02.2016	ORD	ORD	C04	P1001	USD	EA	N	120.00	2
30000017	1	01.03.2016	ORD	ORD	C05	P1002	USD	EA	N	300.00	10
30000018	1	01.04.2016	ORD	ORD	C06	P1003	USD	EA	N	2,400.0	20
30000019	1	01.01.2016	ORD	ORD	C07	P1002	USD	EA	N	900.00	30
30000020	1	01.02.2016	ORD	ORD	C08	P1003	USD	EA	N	120.00	1
30000021	1	01.03.2016	ORD	ORD	C09	P1004	USD	EA	N	14.00	2
30000022	1	01.04.2016	ORD	ORD	C10	P1002	USD	EA	N	90.00	3
30000023	1	01.05.2016	ORD	ORD	C11	P1003	USD	EA	N	480.00	4
30000024	1	01.06.2016	ORD	ORD	C12	P1004	USD	EA	N	35.00	5
50000001	1	01.01.2016	RET	DAMA	C01	P1001	USD	EA	N	300.00	5
50000002	1	01.02.2016	RET	QUAL	C02	P1001	USD	EA	N	120.00	2
50000003	1	01.03.2016	RET	DAMA	C03	P1001	USD	EA	N	600.00	10

Figure 12.36: Data loaded into ZDEMO_O2 and ZDEMO_O3

18. **Query on order data**—Once the composite provider ZDEMO_CP1 is created, create a BEx query on top. This query can be used by the business user to analyze spend. Creation of a query via SAP HANA Studio is discussed next.

   a. Create a new query on ZDEMO_CP1, as shown in Figure 12.37. Right-click on ZDEMO_CP1 and then click NEW • QUERY.

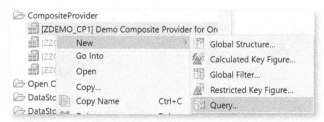

Figure 12.37: Create a query on composite provider

b. On the next screen, give the technical name of the query as ZDEMO_CP1_Q1 and the query description as *Spend Analysis* (as shown in Figure 12.38). Click FINISH.

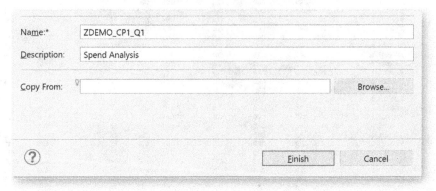

Figure 12.38: Give the technical name and description of the query

c. In the window that opens, click the SHEET DEFINITION Tab, and then right-click on the ROWS section of the screen (as shown in Figure 12.39). Click ADD CHARACTERISTICS.

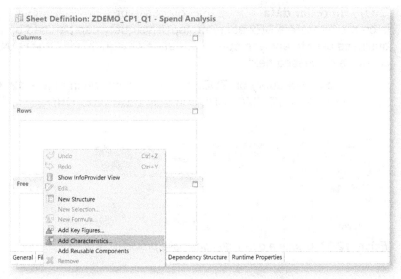

Figure 12.39: Add characteristics to the query definition

d. Add BILLING REGION, BILLING STATE, and CUSTOMER ID. Click OK. This is shown in Figure 12.40.

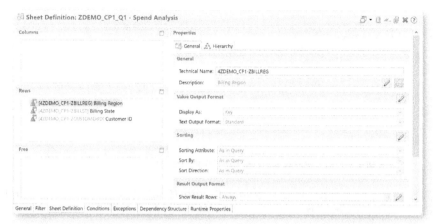

Figure 12.40: Rows section for the query

e. In the COLUMNS section, create two restricted key figures. The first restricted KEY FIGURE (RKF) will have 0AMOUNT, restricted by the ORDER TYPE ORD. The restriction details are shown in Figure 12.41.

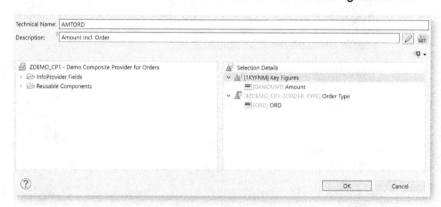

Figure 12.41: First restricted key figure (order value)

f. The second restricted key figure will have the KEY FIGURE 0AMOUNT, but will be restricted by the ORDER TYPE = RET. The restriction details are shown in Figure 12.42.

151

Figure 12.42: First restricted key figure (return value)

g. The final formula is shown in Figure 12.43. It is the NET VALUE and will be AMOUNT INCL. ORDERS – AMOUNT INCL. RET.

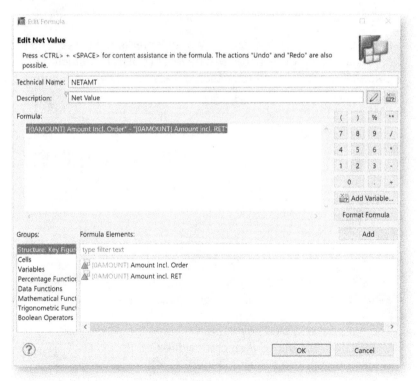

Figure 12.43: Formula for net value

h. Now hide the top two key figures to only see the final formula key figure, which is the NET VALUE.

i. Choose the first and second key figure and change the DISPLAY property from ALWAYS SHOW to ALWAYS HIDE, as shown in Figure 12.44.

Figure 12.44: Hide the first and second key figures

j. Now that the query is available, log on to analysis for office (AO), search for the query (see Figure 12.45), and display the result of the query. AO is a tool given by SAP through which the business users can consume queries to quickly analyze their data.

Figure 12.45: Search for the query using analysis for office (AO)

k. Once the query executes, the result that is displayed is shown in Figure 12.46. The query result shows by region, state, customer, and spend values.

	A	B	C	D
				Net Value
	Billing Region	**Billing State**	**Customer ID**	USD
	MID WEST	ILLINOIS	C01	2,400.00
			C04	180.00
			C07	3,300.00
			C10	180.00
		NEBRASKA	C03	6,100.00
			C06	2,540.00
			C09	134.00
			C12	185.00
	WEST	UTAH	C02	1,220.00
			C05	1,500.00
			C08	127.00
			C11	720.00

Figure 12.46: Customer spend analysis by region

13 Business example 2—actual customer spend compared with plan data

Another example of a data warehouse is given here. The business users usually want to analyze and compare the actuals data with the plan or the budget data that they prepare for the whole year to spend on advertisements. Assume the budget they want to compare is the advertisement budget that they plan to spend by region. Once the business users can compare the actual customer spend data with plan data, they can spend their advertisement budget more judiciously. Usually, the finance department publishes the advertisement budget early in the year. This budget then undergoes changes, depending upon the amount that gets spent by the department and the profit that the company makes. Every month, the finance department publishes a budget, but they do not want to lose visibility to the budget they created at the beginning of the year. They want to retain that in the data warehouse and then compare the various versions of budgets.

Some points to note

1. Use the customer spend data from business example 1 (Section 12).

2. Budget data gets created in spreadsheets. The finance department then publishes the final version, which needs to be uploaded into the data warehouse.

3. Budget data will be loaded into the data warehouse as V1, V2, V3, and up through V12. The calendar year will track the year in which the data was loaded into the warehouse.

4. V1 for calendar year (InfoObject 0CALYEAR) 2018 is the first version of the budget for 2018. The budget is for each month. Each month is indicated by the calendar month InfoObject (0CALMONTH). The version is indicated by the InfoObject 0VERSION.

5. The version for actuals data will be blank.

Solution for business example 2

1. A flatfile (.CSV file) will be used to load plan data into the data warehouse.

2. The flatfile format for the file is given in Table 13.1. A sample data plan to upload into the data warehouse is given in Appendix 15.5.

Field	Datatype	Length	Type of object added
Version	CHAR	3	InfoObject (0VERSION)
Year	CHAR	4	InfoObject (0VERSION)
Month	CHAR	7	InfoObject (0CALMONTH)
Region	CHAR	20	Field
State	CHAR	20	Field
Plan Value	FLTP		InfoObject (0AMOUNT)
Currency	CHAR	3	InfoObject (0CURRENCY)

Table 13.1: Plan data fields to be used in the data warehouse

3. Use the LSA++ diagram from business example 1 and extend it to add the plan to an aDSO. Figure 13.1 shows the LSA++.

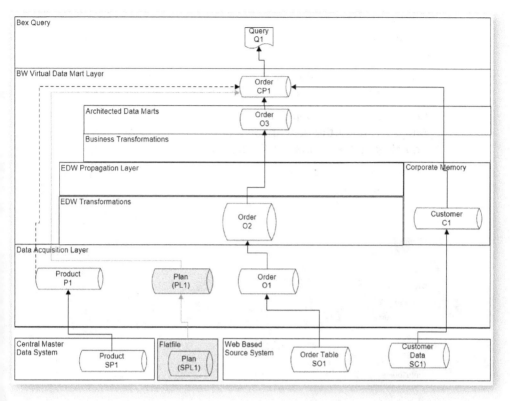

Figure 13.1: LSA++ for business example 2

The components added for plan data are highlighted in light orange. The flatfile, SP1, will be used to load the plan data into aDSO P1. The aDSO P1 will then be connected to the composite provider for reporting purposes. Stage the plan data in P1 and add another aDSO in the EDW transformation layer to perform ETL before connecting it to the ADM layer. This is done to further transform the data. (As I do not need any further transformation for my example, I have connected it from DAL directly into the composite provider.)

4. The aDSO P1 will always contain data that is very small in nature, compared with the order data. Create a query on it to compare different versions of the plan data. Every version will always be loaded once and will never have a delta. So, choose the aDSO of the template model CORPORATE MEMORY—REPORTING CAPABILITIES.

157

5. **Plan data** (ZDEMO_PL1)—The steps below show how to create the aDSO with the template model CORPORATE MEMORY—REPORTING CAPABILITIES.

   a. Right-click on the InfoArea and choose NEW • DATASTORE OBJECT (ADVANCED), as shown in Figure 12.15.

   b. On the screen that pops up, enter the name of the aDSO, *ZDEMO_PL1*, enter the description as *Plan Data for Advertisement,* and click FINISH, (shown in Figure 13.2).

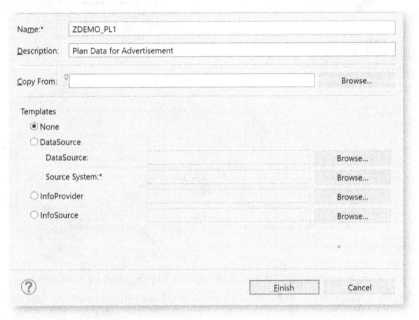

Figure 13.2: Create the plan aDSO

   c. In the next screen, choose the template CORPORATE MEMORY–REPORTING CAPABILITIES and then click APPLY TEMPLATE. The modeling properties get chosen per the selected template, as shown in Figure 13.3.

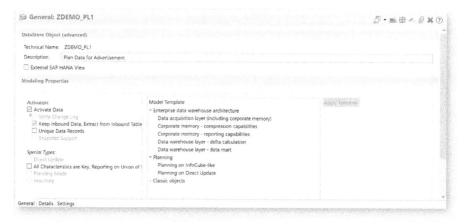

Figure 13.3: Choose the third template for the plan aDSO

d. Click the DETAILS tab. Add the fields as mentioned in the Table 13.2. To add InfoObjects, click *Add InfoObject* and to add fields, click *Add Field*.

Field	Datatype	Length	Type of object added
Version	CHAR	3	InfoObject (0VERSION)
Year	CHAR	4	InfoObject (0VERSION)
Month	CHAR	7	InfoObject (0CALMONTH)
Region	CHAR	20	Field (ZBILLREG)
State	CHAR	20	Field (ZBILLST)
Plan Value	FLTP		InfoObject (0AMOUNT)
Currency	CHAR	3	InfoObject (0CURRENCY)

Table 13.2: Fields for the plan aDSO

159

After adding the fields and InfoObjects, the screen should look like what is shown in Figure 13.4.

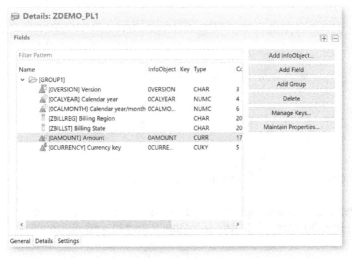

Figure 13.4: Fields for the plan aDSO

e. In the MANAGE KEYS section, add all characters as keys. The keys should look like what is shown in Figure 13.5.

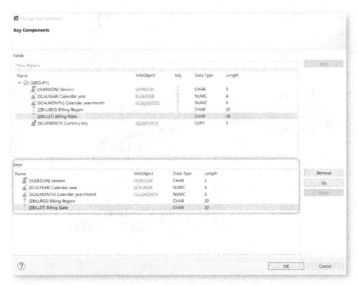

Figure 13.5: Create keys for the plan aDSO

f.   Now activate the aDSO by clicking the ACTIVATE button ( ).

g.   Now that the aDSO is created, load the data. (This load step is not discussed in detail, as this is the same as SAP BW on a non-SAP HANA database.)

6. **Enhance order aDSO ZDEMO_O3**—In order to compare a plan with actuals, the aDSO needs to be enhanced to add two time-related characteristics: 0CALYEAR and 0CALMONTH. Both objects need to be added to the aDSO and derived using 0CALDAY. The enhancement is discussed next.

a.   Find the DSO ZDEMO_O3 and double-click on the aDSO. Click the DETAILS tab. Highlight the ORDERDETAILS group and then click the ADD INFOOBJECT button. Then add the two InfoObjects: 0CALYEAR and 0CALMONTH. The screen should look like what is shown in Figure 13.6.

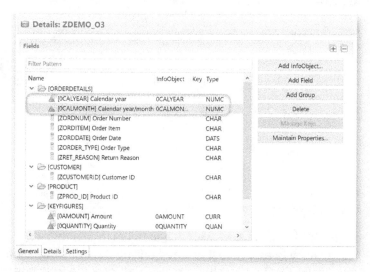

Figure 13.6: Add two time characteristics to the order aDSO

b.   Now activate the aDSO by clicking the ACTIVATE button ( ).

c.   The transformations that load this aDSO need to be reactivated and the 0CALDAY InfoObject needs to be used to populate the newly added objects. Changes to the transformation are shown in Figure 13.7. This is done via the SAP BW administrator work-bench instead of SAP HANA Studio. Now click the ACTIVATE button.

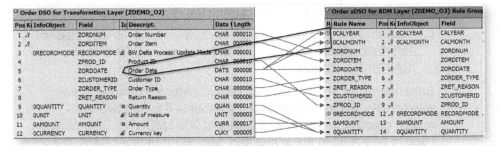

Figure 13.7: Transformation to populate the new InfoObjects

d. While still within the SAP BW administrator workbench, delete the data from aDSO ZDEMO_O3 and repopulate the aDSO ZDEMO_O3. This will help populate the newly added InfoObjects. To drop the data from ZDEMO_O3, right-click on the aDSO and choose DELETE DATA. This is shown in Figure 13.8.

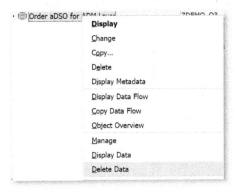

Figure 13.8: Delete data from an aDSO

e. Choose the DTP to load data from ZDEMO_O2 to ZDEMO_O3. That DTP will be inactive as you just finished editing the transformation that feeds ZDEMO_O3. Double-click the DTP, click the EDIT button ( ), and then activate ( ). Now execute the DTP to load data into ZDEMO_O3. To load data, click the EXECUTE tab in the DTP and then click the EXECUTE button.

f. Still within the SAP BW administrator workbench, activate the data in the aDSO. Right-click on the aDSO. Click MANAGE. Then right-click on the last loaded request, and click the ACTIVATE BUTTON.

162

g. Now display data for the aDSO. Right-click on the last loaded request. Choose DISPLAY ACTIVE DATA. Click the EXECUTE button. The added InfoObject, as shown by the yellow highlighting in Figure 13.9, is now populated.

Data Browser: Table /BIC/AZDEMO_O32 Select Entries   27

ZORDNUM	ZORDITE	ZORDDATE	ZORDER_TYPE	ZRET_REASON	ZCUSTOMERI	ZPROD_ID	CURRENC	UNIT	RECORDMODE	CALYEAR	CALMONTH	AMOUNT	QUANTIT
30000001	1	01.01.2016	ORD	ORD	C01	P1001	USD	EA	N	2016	201601	900.00	15
30000002	1	01.02.2016	ORD	ORD	C02	P1001	USD	EA	N	2016	201602	1,200.00	20
30000003	1	01.03.2016	ORD	ORD	C03	P1001	USD	EA	N	2016	201603	5,000.00	100
30000003	2	01.04.2016	ORD	ORD	C04	P1002	USD	EA	N	2016	201604	60.00	2
30000003	3	01.05.2016	ORD	ORD	C05	P1003	USD	EA	N	2016	201605	1,200.00	10
30000003	4	01.06.2016	ORD	ORD	C06	P1004	USD	EA	N	2016	201606	140.00	20
30000007	1	01.07.2016	ORD	ORD	C07	P1005	USD	EA	N	2016	201607	2,400.00	30
30000008	1	01.01.2016	ORD	ORD	C08	P1004	USD	EA	N	2016	201601	7.00	1
30000008	2	01.02.2016	ORD	ORD	C09	P1001	USD	EA	N	2016	201602	120.00	2
30000008	3	01.03.2016	ORD	ORD	C10	P1002	USD	EA	N	2016	201603	90.00	3

Figure 13.9: Added InfoObjects are populated based on order date

7. **Enhance composite provider ZDEMO_CP1**—The composite provider ZDEMO_CP1 needs to be enhanced to add the following objects: the two missing InfoObjects (0CALYEAR and 0CALMONTH) and the plan aDSO. Follow these steps to add the missing elements and plan data:

a. Add the missing InfoObjects—Log back into SAP HANA Studio, find the composite provider, and double-click it. This opens up the object for editing. Click the SCENARIO tab, and then open the group called ORDERDETAILS in the SOURCE section. Highlight the two objects 0CALMONTH *and* 0CALYEAR and drop them into the *ORDERDETAILS* folder in the TARGET section. This completes the addition of the object to the composite provider and also helps map the fields to the source, as shown in Figure 13.10. Now click the ACTIVATE button on the menu bar to activate the InfoObject.

Composite provider activation error

If the composite provider shows an error while activating, replace ZDEMO_O3 with itself. That should resolve the issue. Activate the provider once the replacement is done.

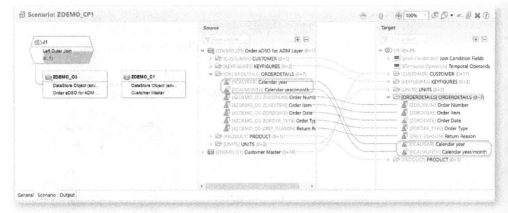

Figure 13.10: Add missing InfoObjects to the composite provider

b. **Add a plan aDSO to the composite provider**—To add the plan aDSO, right-click on the ZDEMO_C3 DSO, and then click UNION WITH, as shown in Figure 13.11.

Figure 13.11: Choose the union with operator to join plan to actuals

c. Highlight UNION OPERATOR U1 and click ADD, as shown in Figure 13.12.

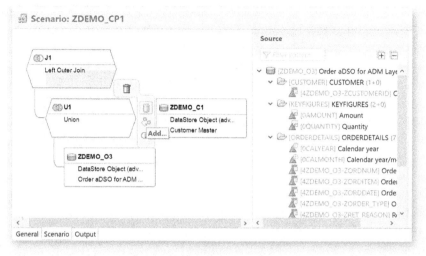

Figure 13.12: Add a part provider to the union

d. Add the aDSO *ZDEMO_PL1* and then click OK, as shown in Figure 13.13.

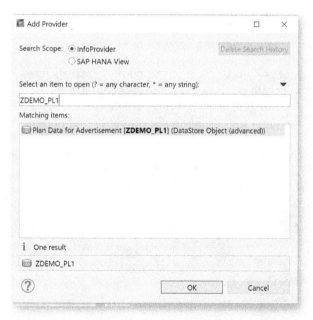

Figure 13.13: Add a plan aDSO to the composite provider

e.   Once the part provider is added, right-click on the part provider in the SOURCE section, and choose CREATE ASSIGNMENTS. This is shown in Figure 13.14. Click on each part provider for the union and then click the CUSTOMER ADSO to choose the source system assignment. Then add the join condition for the left outer join for the CUSTOMER ID. This should rebuild all the assignments between the source and target.

Figure 13.14: Assign fields from a plan aDSO to the composite provider

f.   Click ACTIVATE to activate the composite provider.

8. **Create a new query**—In order to analyze plan vs. actuals, create a query. In order to create a query, copy the existing query ZDEMO_CP1_Q1 into ZDEMO_CP1_Q2. This is shown in Figure 13.15. Follow these steps to enhance the query and add plan details:

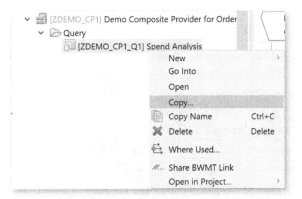

Figure 13.15: Copy a query to create a new query

a. In the screen that pops up, put the query name as *ZDEMO_CP1 _Q2* and enter the description of the query as *Plan vs. Actuals* (see Figure 13.16).

Figure 13.16: Create a new query for plan vs. actuals

b. In the key figure AMOUNT INCL. ORDER, add restriction for 0VERSION = Blank. This is shown in Figure 13.17. This restriction makes sure that the values for this key figure come from the actuals cube.

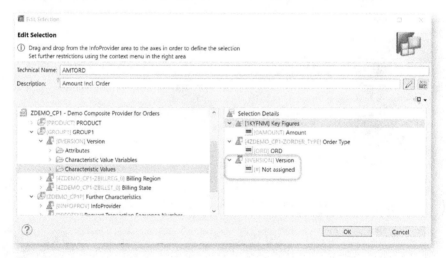

Figure 13.17: Add a blank version to the actuals order key figure

c. In the key figure AMOUNT INCL. RET, add restriction for 0VERSION = Blank. This is shown in Figure 13.18. This restriction makes sure that the values for this key figure come from the actuals cube.

167

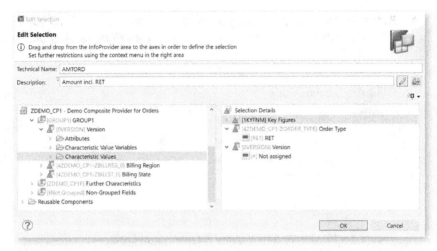

Figure 13.18: Add blank version to the actuals return key figure

d.   Now add a new key figure that has 0AMOUNT and the InfoCube restriction is set to ZDEMO_PL1. This is shown in Figure 13.19.

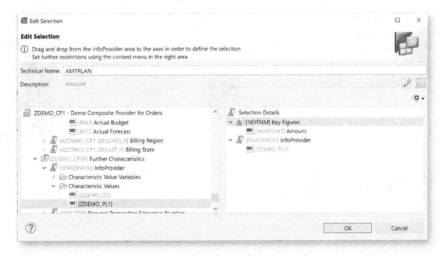

Figure 13.19: Create an amount key figure for plan cube

e.   Rename the key figure to AMOUNT (Plan). Click the SAVE button (⬛) to save the query.

f. Now find the query in AO (as shown in Figure 13.20) and execute the query to display actuals versus plan data via analysis for office.

ZDEMO_CP1_Q	
Description	Technical Name
Plan vs. Actuals	ZDEMO_CP1_Q2
Spend Analysis	ZDEMO_CP1_Q1

Figure 13.20: Choose the plan vs. actuals query in AO

g. After further filtering on the west region, the query shows the results as depicted in Figure 13.21.

A	B	C
	Amount Actuals	Amount Plan
Billing Region	USD	USD
West	20,626.00	30,000.00
Overall Result	**20,626.00**	**30,000.00**

Figure 13.21: Plan vs. actuals

NOTE: Slight adjustments were made to the example to get the query results shown.

169

14 Some more features within SAP BW on HANA

With every upgrade, SAP is improving features that are available within the SAP BW on SAP HANA toolset. More and more modeling features are now available within SAP HANA Studio. Several features that were only available in RSA1 admin workbench are now only available within SAP HANA Studio. We still cannot do away with RSA1 though. We need to still use both RSA1 and SAP HANA Studio together to build BW objects.

With the latest SAP BW 7.5, we can now completely design our queries using SAP HANA Studio. We do not need to use the SAP BEx Query Designer at all. SAP HANA Studio gives an added advantage: we can now preview the data. This flexibility is not available within the query designer tool.

One more flexibility that comes along with SAP BW 7.5 is that the query can be exposed to create SAP HANA views by using the EXTERNAL SAP HANA VIEW checkbox. This will further help to consume the data directly via SQL.

The ABAP used in transformations was originally processed within the application layer. With SAP BW on SAP HANA, this code can now be pushed down to the SAP HANA database for a faster execution. This can be achieved by creating an SAP HANA expert script on transformations.

InfoObjects can now be managed using SAP HANA Studio. SAP HANA Studio gives the flexibility to preview master data with the InfoObject. It also supports INT8 key figures.

Modeling within SAP BW on SAP HANA is getting more exciting with more features being released with every patch level. Welcome to the exciting times!

15 Appendix

15.1 File format

Table 15.1 shows the flat file format for loading order data into the system.

Order Num	Order Item	Product ID	Order Date	Customer ID	Order Qty	Order Value
30000001	1	P1001	20160101	C01	15	239.85
30000002	1	P1001	20160101	C02	20	319.8

Table 15.1: File format for order file

15.2 Customer data

Customer ID	Date of Birth	Gender	Billing Address 1	Billing Address 2	Billing City	Billing State	Billing Region	Shipping Addr	Shipping Ad	Shipping Cit	Shipping State	Shipping Region	Corres	Joining Date	Payment Term
C01	01.01.1970	M	1201 westgate dr		Plainfield	Illinois	Mid West						B	01.01.2011	30
C02	01.01.1971	F	190 tesla state		Park City	Utah	West						B	01.01.2012	30
C03	01.01.1972	M	180 Siena dr		Grand Islar	Nebraska	Mid West						B	01.01.2013	30
C04	01.01.1973	F	1300 pointe dr		Plainfield	Illinois	Mid West						B	01.01.2014	30
C05	01.01.1974	M	1600 grand island		Park City	Utah	West						B	01.01.2015	30
C06	01.01.1975	F	900 broadview dr		Grand Islar	Nebraska	Mid West						B	01.01.2016	30
C07	01.01.1976	M	1900 shamrock st		Plainfield	Illinois	Mid West						B	01.01.2017	30
C08	01.01.1977	F	162 wheeler dr		Park City	Utah	West						B	01.01.2011	30
C09	01.01.1978	M	132 wellington cir		Grand Islar	Nebraska	Mid West						B	01.01.2012	30
C10	01.01.1979	F	165 valero dr		Plainfield	Illinois	Mid West						B	01.01.2013	30
C11	01.01.1980	M	166 Amarilo ctr		Park City	Utah	West						B	01.01.2014	30
C12	01.01.1981	F	190 station road		Grand Islar	Nebraska	Mid West						B	01.01.2015	30

Figure 15.1: File for customer data

15.3 Product data

Product ID	Product Cost
P1001	60
P1002	30
P1003	120
P1004	7
P1005	80

Figure 15.2: Attribute load for product

Product ID	Product Text	Product Text	Product Text
P1001	Kids buggy	Kids buggy	Kids buggy
P1002	Petite Blue Dress with polka dots	Petite Blue Dress with polka dots	Petite Blue Dress with polka dots
P1003	Camping set	Camping set	Camping set
P1004	Lipstick - Red	Lipstick - Red	Lipstick - Red
P1005	Handbag with a small purse	Handbag with a small purse	Handbag with a small purse

Figure 15.3: Text load for product

15.4 Actuals data for orders

Order Num	Order Item	Product ID	Order Date	Customer ID	Order Type	Reason	Order Qty	Order Value
30000001	1	P1001	01.01.2016	C01	Ord	Ord	15	239.85
30000002	1	P1001	01.02.2016	C02	Ord	Ord	20	319.8
30000003	1	P1001	01.03.2016	C03	Ord	Ord	100	1599
30000003	2	P1002	01.04.2016	C04	Ord	Ord	2	60
30000003	3	P1003	01.05.2016	C05	Ord	Ord	10	70
30000003	4	P1004	01.06.2016	C06	Ord	Ord	20	240
30000007	1	P1005	01.07.2016	C07	Ord	Ord	30	389.7
30000008	1	P1004	01.01.2016	C08	Ord	Ord	1	12
30000008	2	P1001	01.02.2016	C09	Ord	Ord	2	31.98
30000008	3	P1002	01.03.2016	C10	Ord	Ord	3	90
30000008	4	P1001	01.04.2016	C11	Ord	Ord	4	63.96
30000012	1	P1002	01.05.2016	C12	Ord	Ord	5	150
30000013	1	P1003	01.06.2016	C01	Ord	Ord	15	105
30000014	1	P1004	01.07.2016	C02	Ord	Ord	20	240
30000015	1	P1004	01.01.2016	C03	Ord	Ord	100	1200
30000016	1	P1001	01.02.2016	C04	Ord	Ord	2	31.98
30000017	1	P1002	01.03.2016	C05	Ord	Ord	10	300
30000018	1	P1003	01.04.2016	C06	Ord	Ord	20	140
30000019	1	P1002	01.01.2016	C07	Ord	Ord	30	900
30000020	1	P1003	01.02.2016	C08	Ord	Ord	1	7
30000021	1	P1004	01.03.2016	C09	Ord	Ord	2	24
30000022	1	P1002	01.04.2016	C10	Ord	Ord	3	90
30000023	1	P1003	01.05.2016	C11	Ord	Ord	4	28
30000024	1	P1004	01.06.2016	C12	Ord	Ord	5	60
50000001	1	P1001	01.01.2016	C01	Ret	Dama	5	239.85
50000002	1	P1001	01.02.2016	C02	Ret	Qual	2	319.8
50000003	1	P1001	01.03.2016	C03	Ret	Dama	10	1599

Figure 15.4: Order transaction data

15.5 Plan data for advertisement spend

Version	Year	month	Region	State	Plan Value	Currency
V1	2016	2016001	Mid West	Illinois	2000	USD
V1	2016	2016001	Mid West	Nebraska	2500	USD
V1	2016	2016001	West	Utah	3000	USD
V1	2016	2016002	Mid West	Illinois	2500	USD
V1	2016	2016002	Mid West	Nebraska	3000	USD
V1	2016	2016002	West	Utah	3500	USD
V1	2016	2016003	Mid West	Illinois	3000	USD
V1	2016	2016003	Mid West	Nebraska	3500	USD
V1	2016	2016003	West	Utah	4000	USD
V1	2016	2016004	Mid West	Illinois	2000	USD
V1	2016	2016004	Mid West	Nebraska	2500	USD
V1	2016	2016004	West	Utah	3000	USD
V1	2016	2016005	Mid West	Illinois	2500	USD
V1	2016	2016005	Mid West	Nebraska	3000	USD
V1	2016	2016005	West	Utah	3500	USD
V1	2016	2016006	Mid West	Illinois	3000	USD
V1	2016	2016006	Mid West	Nebraska	3500	USD
V1	2016	2016006	West	Utah	4000	USD
V1	2016	2016007	Mid West	Illinois	2000	USD
V1	2016	2016007	Mid West	Nebraska	2500	USD
V1	2016	2016007	West	Utah	3000	USD
V1	2016	2016008	Mid West	Illinois	2500	USD
V1	2016	2016008	Mid West	Nebraska	3000	USD
V1	2016	2016008	West	Utah	3500	USD
V1	2016	2016009	Mid West	Illinois	3000	USD
V1	2016	2016009	Mid West	Nebraska	3500	USD
V1	2016	2016009	West	Utah	4000	USD
V1	2016	2016010	Mid West	Illinois	2000	USD
V1	2016	2016010	Mid West	Nebraska	2500	USD
V1	2016	2016010	West	Utah	3000	USD

Plan data   Sheet1   (+)

Figure 15.5: Plan data for advertisement spend

175

ESPRESSO TUTORIALS

You have finished the book.

Sign up for our newsletter!

Want to learn more about new e-books?
Get exclusive free downloads and SAP tips.
Sign up for our newsletter!

Please visit us at *newsletter.espresso-tutorials.com* to find out more.

A References

1. *https://help.sap.com/viewer/ 04030263a0d041309a039fa3ea586720/7.5.3/ en-US/cfb5d33cffbe4602b885c95659b0d78b.html*

2. *https://technet.microsoft.com/en-us/library/ms187518(v=sql.105).aspx*

3. *http://Saplearninghub.plateau.com*

4. *http://help.sap.com*

5. *https://help.sap.com/saphelp_nw74/helpdata/en/25/ 3a8dd2746045ea9b84fedd8b966609/frameset.htm*

6. *https://wiki.scn.sap.com/*

7. *http://www.information-management-architect.com/data-warehouse-principles.html*

8. *http://cdn.ttgtmedia.com/searchDataManagement/downloads/ Data_Warehouse_Design.pdf*

9. *https://docs.oracle.com/javase/tutorial/jdbc/overview/database.html*

10. *https://en.wikipedia.org/wiki/SAP_HANA*

11. *https://help.sap.com/saphelp_nw73ehp1/helpdata/en/4a/ 124597ca771b41e10000000a42189c/frameset.htm*

12. *https://help.sap.com/saphelp_nw73ehp1/helpdata/en/22/ ad6fad96b547c199adb588107e6412/frameset.htm*

B   The Author

Deepa Rawat is a senior consultant for a global consulting company. For the past 17 years, her main area of focus has been SAP BW and more recently, SAP BW on SAP HANA. She has extensive experience implementing and leading SAP BW projects globally. Currently, Ms. Rawat is an SAP BW team lead and leads a team of more than 15 consultants across different projects. She has a degree in Masters in Information Systems from University of Southampton, UK.

C Index

D Disclaimer

This publication contains references to the products of SAP SE.

SAP, R/3, SAP NetWeaver, Duet, PartnerEdge, ByDesign, SAP BusinessObjects Explorer, StreamWork, and other SAP products and services mentioned herein as well as their respective logos are trademarks or registered trademarks of SAP SE in Germany and other countries.

Business Objects and the Business Objects logo, BusinessObjects, Crystal Reports, Crystal Decisions, Web Intelligence, Xcelsius, and other Business Objects products and services mentioned herein as well as their respective logos are trademarks or registered trademarks of Business Objects Software Ltd. Business Objects is an SAP company.

Sybase and Adaptive Server, iAnywhere, Sybase 365, SQL Anywhere, and other Sybase products and services mentioned herein as well as their respective logos are trademarks or registered trademarks of Sybase, Inc. Sybase is an SAP company.

SAP SE is neither the author nor the publisher of this publication and is not responsible for its content. SAP Group shall not be liable for errors or omissions with respect to the materials. The only warranties for SAP Group products and services are those that are set forth in the express warranty statements accompanying such products and services, if any. Nothing herein should be construed as constituting an additional warranty.

More Espresso Tutorials Books

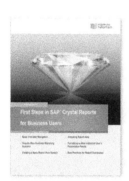

Anurag Barua:

First Steps in SAP® Crystal Reports for Business Users

- ▶ Basic end-user navigation
- ▶ Creating a basic report from scratch
- ▶ Formatting to meet individual presentation needs

http://5017.espresso-tutorials.com

Wolfgang Niefert:

Business Intelligence with SAP® BI Edge

- ▶ Get to know the BI Edge Solutions 4.1
- ▶ Universe, Crystal Reports and Web Intelligence for beginners
- ▶ Learn about Connecting BI with SAP ERP (ECC 6.0)
- ▶ Case study with many screenshots and explanations

http://4040.espresso-tutorials.com

Kermit Bravo & Scott Cairncross:

SAP® Enterprise Performance Management (EPM) Add-In

- ▶ Learn about the Connection Concept
- ▶ Get familiar with the SAP EPM Add-In for Excel and BPC 10.1
- ▶ Create a Basic Report from Scratch
- ▶ Walk through a Detailed Case Study

http://5042.espresso-tutorials.com

Gerardo di Giuseppe:

First Steps in SAP® Business Warehouse (BW)

- ▶ Tips for Loading Data to SAP BW with SAP ETL
- ▶ Using Business Content to Accelerate your BW objects
- ▶ How to Automate ETL Tasks Using Process Chains
- ▶ Leverage BEx Query Designer and BEx Analyzer

http://5088.espresso-tutorials.com

Jörg Böke:

SAP® BI Analysis Office – a Practical Guide

▶ Installation and prerequisites

▶ Analysis Excel Pivot, Ribbon and Context Menu Explained

▶ Enhanced reporting with API and Visual Basic (VBA)

▶ Comparison between Analysis Office AO and BEx

http://5096.espresso-tutorials.com

Shreekant Shiralkar & Deepak Sawant:

SAP® BW Performance Optimization

▶ Use BW statistics effectively

▶ Leverage tools for extraction, loading, modeling and reporting

▶ Monitor performance using the Workload Monitor & database statistics

▶ Use indexes to understand key elements of performance

http://5102.espresso-tutorials.com

Christian Savelli:

SAP® BW on SAP HANA

▶ Tips for upgrading, maintaining, and running BW on HANA

▶ Data loading methods and real-time data acquisition

▶ New reporting paradigm for BW on HANA

▶ HANA data architecture

http://5128.espresso-tutorials.com

Frank Riesner, Klaus-Peter Sauer:

First Steps in SAP® FI Configuration

▶ Migration, sizing, operation, data management with SAP BW/4HANA and SAP BW 7.5 on HANA

▶ The new central source Systems SAP HANA and ODP

▶ New modeling options, mixed scenarios, LSA++, and differences compared to SAP BW 7.5

▶ The role of BW in operational SAP reporting

http://5215.espresso-tutorials.com

www.ingramcontent.com/pod-product-compliance
Lightning Source LLC
Chambersburg PA
CBHW071124050326
40690CB00008B/1333